Credulous

 **MISSIONAL WISDOM LIBRARY**
RESOURCES FOR CHRISTIAN COMMUNITY

The Missional Wisdom Foundation experiments with and teaches about alternative forms of Christian community. The definition of what constitutes a Christian community is shifting as many seek spiritual growth outside of the traditional confines of church. Christians are experimenting with forming communities around gardens, recreational activities, coworking spaces, and hundreds of other focal points, connecting with their neighbors while being aware of the presence of God in their midst. The Missional Wisdom Library series includes resources that address these kinds of communities and their cultural, theological, and organizational implications.

Series Editor: Larry Duggins

> vol. 1: *Missional. Monastic. Mainline.: A Guide to Starting Missional Micro-Communities in Historically Mainline Traditions*, by Elaine A. Heath and Larry Duggins
>
> vol. 2: *Simple Harmony: Thoughts on Holistic Christian Life*, by Larry Duggins and Elaine A. Heath
>
> vol. 3: *Together: Community as a Means of Grace*, by Larry Duggins
>
> vol. 4: *What Kind of God?: Reading the Bible with a Missional Church*, by Bret Wells

Forthcoming titles
> *The Julian Way: Towards a Theology of Fullness for All of God's People*, by Justin Hancock
>
> *Virtuous Friendship: The New Testament, Grego-Roman Friendship Language, and Contemporary Community*, by Douglas A. Hume

Credulous

A Journey Through Life,
Faith, and the Bulletin

Andrea L. Lingle

 CASCADE *Books* • Eugene, Oregon

CREDULOUS
A Journey Through Life, Faith, and the Bulletin

Missional Wisdom Library: Resources for Christian Community 5

Copyright © 2018 Andrea L. Lingle. All rights reserved. Except for brief quotations in critical publications or reviews, no part of this book may be reproduced in any manner without prior written permission from the publisher. Write: Permissions, Wipf and Stock Publishers, 199 W. 8th Ave., Suite 3, Eugene, OR 97401.

Cascade Books
An Imprint of Wipf and Stock Publishers
199 W. 8th Ave., Suite 3
Eugene, OR 97401

www.wipfandstock.com

PAPERBACK ISBN: 978-1-5326-1548-1
HARDCOVER ISBN: 978-1-5326-1550-4
EBOOK ISBN: 978-1-5326-1549-8

Cataloguing-in-Publication data:

Names: Lingle, Andrea L., author.

Title: Credulous : a journey through life, faith, and the bulletin / Andrea L. Lingle.

Description: Eugene, OR: Cascade Books, 2018 | Series: Missional Wisdom Library: Resources for Christian Community 5 | Includes bibliographical references.

Identifiers: ISBN 978-1-5326-1548-1 (paperback) | ISBN 978-1-5326-1550-4 (hardcover) | ISBN 978-1-5326-1549-8 (ebook)

Subjects: LCSH: Christian biography. | Spiritual life—Christianity.

Classification: BX5995.L56 A3 2018 (print) | BX5995.L56 A3 (ebook)

All quotations used by permission.

Material from *School(s) of Conversion* used by permission of Wipf and Stock Publishers, www.wipfandstock.com.

All biblical references are from the New Revised Standard Version, copyright © 1989, Division of Christian Education of the National Council of the Churches of Christ in the United States of America. Used by permission. All rights reserved.

Manufactured in the U.S.A. 04/03/18

To my husband, who unceasingly creates
space for me to share my voice.

Jesus said, *"Let the little children come to me, and do not stop them; for it is to such as these that the kingdom of heaven belongs."*

—MATTHEW 19:14

Contents

Preface / ix

Acknowledgments / xi

Introduction / xiii

1 Prelude / 1
2 Call to Worship / 4
3 Welcome and Greeting / 11
4 Hymn—Nothing but the Blood / 25
5 Creed / 39
6 Anthem—Sing Me to Heaven / 47
7 Prayer of the People / 53
8 Offering / 64
9 Doxology / 81
10 Children's Time / 88
11 Scripture Reading—John 1:1–5 / 97
12 Sermon / 103
13 Communion / 109
14 Benediction / 117

Bibliography / 119

Preface

Hello. My name is Andrea. I wrote this book.

I wrote this book because I wanted to: I wanted to see if I could, I wanted to share what I see, I wanted to spark questions, and, most of all, I wanted to do so as a lay person. I am a lay theologian. To be a lay theologian is to make two claims: there is a God about which I think and there are many perspectives from which to do so. There is the academic. There is the ordained. There is the lay. Without a balance between perspectives the God we are all seeing flattens into a cartoon. It is only through the interplay between study, authority, and wonder that the ineffable can begin to emerge.

This book was written every afternoon for a year during naptime. It was written in gardens and my imagination. It was written, one moment at a time, and that is the way faith is for me. I will be sitting, exactly where my planner says I should be, trying to parse out Important Ideas, and suddenly tiny handprints on the walls of the church will turn my head around. There! There is God. The church is all aged granite, serious and profound, and there on one of the columns carved into the facade are two twin handprints, thumbs almost touching, perfect in their impertinence—a reminder that incarnation is sweaty, dirty, and invasive.

I'm a retro-church hipster. I went to church after it was cool. I grew up in the church, traded in memory verses for social justice, traded in religion for atheism, and then realized that the whole thing is something else entirely, all while going to church, for life.

Preface

So, I thought it would be retro-church hipster to write a book about contemplative theology using a church bulletin as a framework. I know, right?!

Just in case you aren't familiar, a church bulletin is the folded piece of paper the ushers (people standing at the doors) hand you as you walk in so you know what happens when and have a place to put your gum.

The only problem with writing a church book right now is the church scene is a bit untidy. There is senseless argument and decline and bureaucracy. Now that it is no longer cool or assumed that a person would be in church on Sunday morning, there seems to be an impulse to explain why one still goes. But I don't know how to explain. I am moderately afraid I go out of habit. What interests me is, amid the clamor of arguments and definitions, a quiet pulse of hope that faith and spirituality can be resurrected toward a new way of joy and peace. If we could let go of truth and take hold of mystery, what would we see? If we could abandon our obligation for curiosity, where would we go? If we could see each other in the light of infinite abundance, what would we do?

So, let's wander in and out of the lines of the Sunday morning bulletin. Let's stand at the door of the church and wonder about the emptying pews and our own aching hearts. Let's use the creeds, the hymns, the prayers, and the people to set ourselves a-wondering about the world, faith, and life.

Acknowledgments

I would like to formally thank my children, who are my teachers in all things; Larry Duggins for giving me the opportunity to share these words; my parents, who are always present in my mind; all the people who kept my children to give me time to write; and my dog, Jessie, who never left my side—not once, not ever.

Introduction

My husband, Luke, and I got married in June 2004, and in August Luke started divinity school at Duke University in Durham, North Carolina. We were fresh-faced and young. We made friends, went to basketball games, and learned a whole new language for faith. I had a Duke University Spouse ID card. All my friends did too. We knew that once we were let loose on the world, church reform would begin spreading like smiles. The church would not be able to withstand our gentle but firm redirection.

Apparently, someone had already tried gentle but firm redirection. Also: pleading, bribery, guilt, shame, and cookies. And still the church heads toward stagnancy and bureaucratic malaise and we with it. Here we are, trees planted by the stream of our choice, withering. And we have been promised that that was the one thing we wouldn't do.

We are United Methodists. Luke was a "first career" pastor, and I always referred to his appointments as "our" ministry. Technically, there was the year that I was the music director at his church and it was our ministry, but, mostly, I was the eager-puppy type—trotting alongside with my leash in my mouth, absurdly proud of how much I was helping. And we were trotting right along for a while, then we slowed to a walk, and now we are just hoping that the detour signs lead somewhere.

People everywhere are leaving church. When asked why, most say there is nothing in church for them; they are spiritual but not religious, and the church is not relevant. There is a rising sense of dissatisfaction with "truth traditions,"[1] or religions that claim to have a singular, exclusive truth. The "Nones," the group of people who select "none" for "religious affiliation," now have a cultural identity. They are unaffiliated, not uninterested. Or not all of them are uninterested.

For two years, Luke was a Church Vitality Strategist. His job was to go into a church, do some diagnostics, and make a plan to increase the church's vitality. The plan was to have him work with as many churches as possible, but the reality was he was called into the churches that were dying. Churches that were refusing to live. After his assessment, he would talk to his team and make a recommendation. Sometimes that recommendation was to close the church. No church was ever closed. Because the vision of the church is to stay alive. Stay alive at all costs. Even if your indicator for success, the weekly attendance, indicates you should close.

The church may be called to do God's work, but it never goes anywhere but back to committee. Back and forth. Always planning to do something while empty, aging buildings become megaliths.

The church we serve was built almost one hundred years ago.

Aside: The trouble with discussing religion and spirituality is that the words we use are full of guilt and shame. If you grew up in the church, you undoubtedly sprawled, in forced stillness and quiet, on the floor at the front of the sanctuary and were asked this question: is the church the building or the people? Of course the child-you, if you had been there long enough, knew that the answer was "the people," but there was always that kid who let the horrifying truth slip out into that sacred space: the church is the building. Who *doesn't* think of it that way?

> *Here is the church and here is the steeple.*
> *Open it up and see all the people.*

It's a language problem. You simply never think: here *are* the church. We have homophones with baggage.

Okay. Sorry.

---

1. This is a term that I heard in an interview with the former head rabbi of the United Kingdom, Jonathan Sacks.

Introduction

In the particular old building where we gather with our worshipping community (there . . . fixed it), the hilly terrain and the many phases of construction have rendered the building somewhat bewildering. For example, if you wanted to get from the nursery to the youth room, you can take two flights of stairs or an elevator from the first floor to the third floor. Then you have to walk from the education wing, through the offices, down a few steps into the original education wing, and then up another flight of stairs.

The stairs from the nursery to the third floor are an industrial stairwell. Echo-y cinderblock stairs with pipe handrails. The ones that make you feel like you could grab both hand rails and slide down like the hero, fugitive, gymnast you are. I can get my feet off the floor, but I can never slide. Maybe I need chalk.

The stairwell has large picture windows on the second- and third-floor landings overlooking the memorial garden. The second floor is ground level in that section of the building and the window is filled with a stained-glass picture of an apple tree. I think the tree is supposed to be depicting the seasons because one section has blossoms and two have fruit. It bothers me.

There is no winter.

No winter?

Winter. It is nature's liminal space. A liminal space is rest, reflection, suffering, hunger, stillness, discomfort. Winter is important. It gives the beset gardener a chance to catch up—to mulch, to prune, to plan. Winter is dark. The birds fly away, the leaves blow away, the animals sleep. Gone is the hilarity of watermelon and tomato and cucumber, those watery fruits of summer, too delicate to preserve in their freshness. Now comes resolute stew. Broths thick with onion and garlic and bone. We need this in the winter. It is a difficult time.

It is winter for the Christian church. A time of decline. The church has been around for almost two thousand years and there are cycles of growth and decline.[2] Its history is a tumble of the best and worst of what humanity is. Because the church is the people.

---

2. Tickle, *Great Emergence*.

Introduction

Many are beginning to ask if the church is dying. Things are moving downward: membership, ordination, giving. But all things look like they are dying in the winter.

In her book *The Mystic Way of Evangelism*, Elaine Heath talks about this season as a "dark night of the soul," quoting St. John of the Cross. Heath goes on to say that "the fruit of the night is about the transformation of relationships into expressions of love of God and neighbor, and love of self for the sake of God."[3] This gives me hope. But it is a tentative hope. I have no doubt that the eternal, uncreated, triune God will endure, but will we?

Winter isn't a nap. It is a life-and-death struggle. Things die in the winter. Winter is cold and sharp and dangerous. The grain of a tree holds the marks of the dark and cold. Ring upon ring. At first those rings are small, but each year they expand. Apparently, there are those who can look at the rings on a tree and tell things about the past. *Eighty years ago the cold was harsh and lasted much longer than normal. Ten years ago the cold never truly came.* Dark, light, dark, light, cold, hot, cold, hot. This is the way of things.

Yes, the Christian church is in a liminal space right now. It is awkward. Exposed. Vulnerable. Dangerous. So many things could happen. So many things could be lost. Like in a garden, there are ways to encounter winter that will encourage growth and ways that will simply kill the plants. Fortunately, there is wisdom to seek out. Winter has come before.

Paul Tillich says this in his book *The Courage to Be*: "striving towards self-preservation or towards self-affirmation makes a thing be what it is."[4] If Tillich is correct, then there is power in the act of intending. But, does that mean that if the pews are empty or the healing doesn't happen the intention was faulty? Because that sounds a lot like guilt and shame. For Tillich, what is resonant is the striving to become, not what you become. It seems that what we are called to do is to try.

But, why?

---

3. Heath, *Mystic Way of Evangelism*, 30.
4. Tillich, *Courage to Be*, 21.

Introduction

There is a lifetime's worth of questions here. I seem to need to wander with them, to look at them, pick them up, turn them over and watch their little legs wave around in the air, perhaps taste a few, and, hopefully, come away different.

1

Prelude

SIMON WAS A FISHERMAN, and it had been a bad night for fishing. He would be taking nothing home that morning. Nothing to sell, nothing to eat, nothing to say. He had finished mending his nets and sat, thinking about what he would tell his wife. The useless ropes, coiled neatly beneath his feet, mocked his need. "We will not provide for you," they sneer, "we will just require everything from you."

There is a story in the Gospel of Luke, chapter 5, wherein Jesus is teaching on the edge of a lake. A lake with a sea complex. There were a lot of people and Jesus decided to get into a boat to give himself some space and (says my husband who has been there) make use of the natural amplification of the water. He got into Simon's boat and pushed off the shore of the Sea of Galilee.

Jesus interrupted Simon's routine: fish, mend, sleep. Jesus climbed into his boat without asking. Simon looked up from his thoughts, startled by this intrusive stranger. The shallow boat rocked back and forth as the man pushed it off the shore, jumped

CREDULOUS

in, and turned to talk to a gathering of people who had followed him to the shore. Simon sat, transfixed by the oddity of the moment. The man was teaching the people about a kingdom of God. It made Simon uncomfortable. It would be dangerous if the Romans overheard.

Then the man stopped talking. He spoke a blessing on the people and turned to face Simon. "Throw your nets into the deep water," the man said.

The deep water. It is the place where things happen.

Simon looked down at the fickle, freshly mended nets. He was tired. He had been out all night and had nothing to show for it. It seemed impossible—hauling his nets back out would take more energy than he had. But, he didn't want to go home. His children would be hungry. So, he rowed skeptically out to the deep water.

The nets rumbled down the side of the boat. Simon hadn't even thrown them. He just let them slide over the edge, watching as the wooden floats stretched away from him. Then they all began to disappear. First the ones at the far end, then each in succession, nearing the boat. The boat began to tip while Simon clung to a net bulging with more fish than he could manage. Jesus stood next to Simon, pulling inexpertly on the writhing nets, shouting with glee.

Later in the New Testament, in John's Gospel, the disciples are gathered on the shore of the same lake. They have been through a Story, but the ending stumped them. The hero didn't win. The hero didn't even fight. So, they gathered on the edge of the land.

"I'm going fishing," Peter said. Jesus had changed everything, even his name. He got into his boat and pushed off shore, not even looking at the rest of the men who scrambled to join him. Peter reached over his head and pulled his tunic off and folded it deliberately. Over the last three years he had lost the corded muscle of a fisherman. He was thin now. Thin, confused, and sad. And he was still tired. He grunted with the effort of lifting his net and his mind

Prelude

began to relax. He knew these motions. Twist, heave, release, pull. There weren't any fish, but he almost didn't care. This was where Jesus had found him. He let his mind wander as sweat began to run down his arms and drip from his elbows. There had been so many moments with Jesus when Peter had felt something happening. He had stood on water, he had seen the water calmed, and then he had felt the splash of blood and water when the soldier had emptied Jesus's watery lungs after he had given up.

He shouted with effort as he flung the net out as far as it would go. His voice broke and he felt tears mixing with the sweat on his face.

Some guy called easily from the shore. "Hey, catching anything?" They hadn't bothered to go out too far.

"No," the other men replied.

"Try the other side." Peter's face flushed with anger and embarrassment.

"Right," he said, dragging the net carelessly across the boat and tossing it belligerently into the water. Suddenly, the net heaved with fish. Peter shouted to the others to help him. He turned his head to look at the man on the beach, and there he was, with that stupid smirk on his face. Jesus. Peter grabbed his tunic, yanked it over his head, and dove in.

Yet another fishing story. The parallels could not be more obvious, but this time the solution is completely different. Try the other side. Try something new. Personally, I hate fishing, but I get the frustration of trying to do something that should work but doesn't. I came, I sweated, I cried, and nothing happened. So, what is the right way? Go deep or try something new? I feel like my net has been empty for a while. I am left wondering what to do next while mending what isn't working. Is Jesus, the inexpressible God incarnate, calling us into the depths or to the other side? Is sliding into the pew, just as the last notes of the Prelude fade, helping me hear the voice of he who calls from the shore, or is the liturgy I love just distracting me?

2

Call to Worship

I sit in the pew feeling uncomfortable. It is hard and too slippery. I sit, trying to keep myself from slumping, absurdly, onto the floor. There is someone up there talking. Praying or preaching or singing or whatever, but I am falling, in slow motion, off my seat; sliding, ignominiously, onto the floor. I cross my legs at the knee, and shove my foot against the pew rack.

I am wedged.

But now the pew rack is protesting—bending in and looking indignant. So, I sit up, straight up, with my back off the pew so I am balanced. I am no longer falling, but now I am conspicuous. Stabbing up from my seat like a startled bunny, ready to stand and flee. So, I settle back down and tuck my foot under the pew rack. It doesn't help as much, but I can be cool about it. "What's wrong?" my husband asks.

"Nothing, why?"

"You're twitchy."

"Sorry."

I am twitchy. Preoccupied with staying in my seat. Apparently, my act of worship is not falling on the floor. Has it come to this? Has the devotion of thirty-five years of Christian practice been reduced to balancing on a slippery oak pew?

Perhaps.

Church and I have come to an impasse. I am here, but there is an echo inside me.

Truthfully, there is an echo within the walls of the church too. Something has changed. Something is missing. Things seems hollow. The hymns that once seemed so resonant ricochet off the walls. The prayers seem a scripted performance. The offering plate seems demanding.

Is there another way? Is there a wisdom beyond my discomfort? I have seen the manifestos of those who have abandoned the church. Should I publish my exit papers and join the protest? I sit here wrestling with modern Christianity, and I don't know why. Walking away would be easier.

This morning I took a star-lit walk around my cul-de-sac. I walk in my cul-de-sac because I walk before my children wake up so I have to be within earshot of the house just in case someone has a bad dream. I walk in starlight because it fills me with wonder.

Twinkle, twinkle little star,
How I wonder what you are.

How I do wonder. There they are, spread out across the sky like dew drops, thunderous fits of exploding gas so hot that they burn you from ninety-two million miles away. A star is an echo of ongoing violence. It is a dance of power so radically giant and kinetic that the light-noise of its stomping feet travels out into the universe for thousands of years.

Star,
    twinkle, twinkle, indeed.

CREDULOUS

From this distance, millennia away, stars are safe. An object of mindful meditation to prepare a mother for a day with noisy children. Nothing to worry about.

I feel an echo inside me. An echo of thunderous feet, pounding out the pulse of the universe. Something sings to me from the stars, and perhaps that same voice sings to me from the broken, violent, moldering heap of religion. I wonder if it is a muse or a siren.

I have read stories of people who have given themselves, down to their toenails, to a faith that tethered them to a burning stake. I sense that those with their feet in the fire went for a purpose and fear that purpose might have been forgotten or lost. I think it goes by the same name as that which pins me in a pew, but I don't understand how that which I experience on Sunday morning could compel someone to self-annihilation.

My pillow is dappled with the remains of tears. I am overwhelmed by the sadness of being unable to stay or leave. Is my spirit too frail to risk either faith or doubt? I feel it must take boldness I don't have to embrace faith or admit that life is an accidental experiment in probability. I have been overtaken by the thing I dread most: cowardice. The failure to be who you see yourself to be.

Here I am, squirming and uncomfortable. Unable to find my equilibrium in church: the oak and organ edition. And I love oak and organ. I love liturgy. I have a distinct thing for vestments. But these waters of faith, once deep and sustaining, have withered into shallow puddles, fruitless and unsatisfying. And I don't even know if it's them or me. Although, since I seem to always find a parking space, it's not just me.

Church is declining. I have read the studies and listened to the interviews. I know church is declining. I even understand why, mostly, but I do not know why it is declining for me. I have always found my identity in my faith. I am a person of faith.

I wonder if it just the effect of becoming an adult. I have lost my imagination along with my naiveté. Religion has been revealed as a social construct, used, for the most part, to justify the exploitation of those not in power. I have learned too much. I don't know where to hang my beliefs.

"You should know where to hang your beliefs," the hymns berate. "Hang them there on our holy hill. Hang them there, lifted high and painted red."

I sigh. I am tired of being a person of the cross. I am tired of blood and violence. I am tired of wearing a symbol of torture around my neck and claiming that God loves me and I love God.

I want to be a person of something else.

I want to be a person *of* something else, not on my way *to* something else. I am tired of arranging my theological furniture in just the proper way without knowing how my process theology helps stop my children from bickering or how the quadrilateral heals a broken life.

I am here, called to worship. I know how this will go. I have done all of this before: the creeds, the responses, the anthems and prayers. I will stand up, grateful for a moment of reprieve from the struggle to sit, and the words of the ancient creed will begin to buzz all around me.

I believe in God the Father Almighty, Maker of heaven and earth. All the sibilants and fricatives make a tapestry of sound around me. My mouth stops moving. Do I believe in God? Can I stand and affirm that, yes, I believe in God? How does one do such a thing? How does one believe in God? Religions revel in abstraction, and (or for) it is much easier to discuss the abstract than to engage with it. Love is abstract. God is abstract. I guess God isn't really abstract, but God is so indefinable that God is, to me, abstract. I don't know that I love God. I say I do, but who can claim that they love the indescribable?

CREDULOUS

I do not understand God. It is my suspicion that no one does. God has been named and described in so many ways, it seems there must be general confusion on the topic. Because of our need to quantify and predict the Divine, the transcendent Divine has been named, assigned a role, and, through this disassembly, become finite and tangible. Father. Savior. Provider. King. Lord.

Words are powerful, but names have greater power. If you do not know this, you should find a reasonable fantasy novel and educate yourself. When we name God we always cast God into an image we create of God. Naming God, Father Almighty, or anything else, immediately creates an anti-God. What God isn't. When God is cast into the image of the image, God is flattened. If God is the Father, God is not the Mother.

"It's just a metaphor," you scream. "You are willfully missing the point."

I understand metaphor. I love metaphor. Using metaphor to talk about God is the only avenue we have, but it can be taken too far. Metaphor does not contain that which we talk about; it is simply a rough woodcut illustration. If God is reduced to that which I can name, is God still God?

The creed ends and the Gloria Patri[1] hangs in the air, so sure of itself, so confident about the nature of God: unchangeable and masculine. Amen, amen.

Maybe that is why I squirm in an increasingly empty pew. There is no uncertainty left. In a tradition that is built on mystery and impossibility (incarnation and resurrection), a preponderance of church history centers around defining and protecting what we believe. You don't have to search diligently to find evidence that somehow Christianity has become a tradition of power, control, and fear, and to maintain the proper ethos it has preached a gospel of scarcity.

1. Glory be to the Father,
And to the Son,
And to the Holy Ghost.
As it was in the beginning,
Is now, and ever shall be,
World without end, Amen. Amen.

There is only room for my way.
My understanding.
We will burn yours.
And you. Because you are dangerous.

Historically, religion of all cants has been used for control. Great stories of faith and identity have become litmus tests. If you do this or renounce that, you are with us. We are not content to allow the mystical to be a vague shroud and relinquish the details to a ubiquitous God. We demand to know that our interpretation of a cosmic, timeless, uncreated being is correct. Not just correct, but exclusively so. We have surrounded ourselves with walls made of red letters. And now our walls are growing more and more empty, and we sit in our slippery, spacious pews, wondering why. We point backwards to a time we do not inhabit, and think that that moment, that unrecoverable moment, is where we need to be. If we could only go back to when the pews were full and the covered dish suppers were well attended, then life would be good.

American Christianity has enough if-then's to amply fill a swimming pool. If people came, if Sunday morning were sacred, if the music were more relevant, if parking were more straightforward, if Sunday school were more engaging, then our churches would be full. But to what end? What is it all for?

The choir begins the Anthem. I ponder the great mysteries of the ages as the music lifts me out of my common mind into the realm of the sublime. Or, I have kids and I spend the entire time of hushed, polite quiet trying to silently manage their squirming bodies. They know. They know I am trapped in the middle of hundreds of people and exposed by quiet. I am powerless to follow through on any of the threats my eyebrows imply. How is it

CREDULOUS

possible that folding the bulletin into a paper airplane is roughly as loud as a Def Leppard concert?

Now my daughter is up and dancing in the aisle. I debate. Should I make her sit down or join her? There are the stars, twinkling and filling me with wonder. There are the leaves of autumn burning with color and flinging themselves into the wind. For them, one last dance is worth the risk of leaping from the branch. I feel that there should be dancing, but I worry that it is just histrionics. Look at me! See! I am spiritual! I suddenly wish I could be six again. When I was six, dancing was just dancing. Sure, I wanted to be seen, I wanted to be adored, but that is what six-year-olds do. And we adore them, never once accusing them of acting out of their ego.

After a few minutes, I make her sit down. I am a coward.

Sitting there, abs clenched, staring at the pew in front of me, I realize: if I stay in the pew, I need to let the dancing back in. Not to save the church. Not as a reformer. The church seems to be in dire need of rescue, but, truthfully, the church has been here before. I haven't. I haven't seen the numbers dwindle like this. I haven't felt division like this. I haven't felt malaise like this.

I need to let the dancing back in.

3

Welcome and Greeting

WELCOME!
We are so glad you are here!

Did you know that it is impossible to truly fake a smile? Apparently, there are two muscles in your face that you can't access when you are faking a smile. And the church has been faking smiles for a long time now.

I have been in meetings wherein church members moan and berate themselves and each other because there had been a visitor to whom no one spoke. Of course no one spoke to them. No one knew them. It is weird and cheap to welcome a complete stranger in with a smile. Would you do that in your house? If you did, it would be a fake smile.

Because relationship takes time. The church should offer hospitality. Obviously. But, hospitality is different than relationship. The Welcome and Greeting stands in the tension between hospitality and relationship, and neither can be faked or rushed. The church must welcome in the stranger and allow that it will be awkward for everyone until the stranger becomes known. Christian community, Christian relationship, must draw in those who are relationship clumsy, relationship encumbered, relationship impaired, and be willing to live in the discomfort of unfamiliarity. Christian community must commit to hospitality—welcoming in the stranger—and relationship—creating spaces where people become deeply known. Going out and drawing in. Reaching out and opening up. The Welcome and Greeting stands at the beginning of the worship service as a marker that this is the time that we are urged to go further in.

Jesus was sitting in the corner with a few of his friends. They were talking about the things that young men talk about at weddings. His back was against one wall and the cushion beneath him was rolled in half under his side. One arm draped over his knee and from his callused fingers hung an empty mug. There was a chip in the lip on one side and the stain on the bottom was barely sticky. More water than wine.

Jesus looked up and saw a familiar form hurrying through the people milling around. He slid down the wall a little.

"Jesus." Mary's shadow was splayed in triplicate over Jesus's feet. The oil lamps were still burning well.

"Yes, ma'am?"

"Jesus, the wine is gone, and people are starting to complain."

"Mom, what am I supposed to do about that?"

"You can do something." The look on her face was a mixture of pride and stubbornness. "We can all do something." Her voice sounded triumphant.

"I have no idea how to fix that. I am not sure that wine is my deal," he said in a frantic whisper. Jesus has risen to his feet and looked down at the fully decided woman with consternation. "I've never even made wine."

"As if that matters. You, there, follow this man and do as he says." Her voice lifted with confidence as she pointed to a servant hovering at the door near the wash basin.

Welcome and Greeting

Welcome and Greeting does not always go smoothly. Sometimes it feels awkward and exactly like being asked to turn water into wine.

Four years ago, I moved to Asheville, North Carolina, where I encountered Haywood Street Congregation, a church that gives those on the margins a voice. I hesitate to write that out that way, because simply naming people as marginal creates a space between us that is both unhealthy and artificial.

Sick	Well
Alcoholic	Workaholic
Poor	Wealthy
Uneducated	Educated
Meek	Pharisee
Human	Human

There is a temptation to go as a socially normative person into communities that are less so with a degree of condescension. We, the educated, homed, unaddicted, are here to fix the uneducated, unhomed, addicts. Many times people who suffer from homelessness, addiction, or illiteracy certainly would like to not be homeless, addicted, or illiterate, but when *We* come to heal *Them* the subtext of superiority cheapens our relationship.

Superiority is the message of the Pharisee, the Roman, and the Colonizer. We have a right, because of our superior civilization, to demand that you assimilate to us. Our civilization is built on exploitation of people to support a level of individuality and affluence that is killing us and our planet. Jesus's message is radically different. There is enough for everyone to have abundant life as long as we sell all we have and give it to the poor.

CREDULOUS

Haywood Street Congregation is a place where there is space for everyone to speak. The addicts, homeless, women, children, articulate, high, hungry, obese, distracted, skeptical, angry, sad, and lonely all have a voice.

For a vulnerable community, Welcome and Greeting is risky. For all they know, I, the interloper with clean hair, could decide to come with judgment or bring an offering only to abandon them when I become tired. I guessed what it meant for me to be there, and I wanted to honor their trust. I needed this. I needed a place where I could sit on a pew without the label of pastor's wife or mom or daughter. So I sat, a caricature of middle-class motherhood, and struggled to find a way to fit in. Altering my appearance to match seemed tempting, but simply mussing my hair and taking off my shoes seemed hollow. Disrespectful.

"Do not despise the poor, because they will be with you always."[1]

I thought Jesus snapped off this rejoinder in response to criticism about a broken woman adorning her worship with the greatest treasure she had, but maybe he was tired to death of having to explain the obvious and wanted to savor a rare, kind touch before he made his final disastrous journey to Jerusalem.

When Mary poured out her life savings onto his tired and dusty feet, the smell of the costly oil filled the house. She, desperate to be heard over the thunder of the all-male Jewish choir growling out recitatives of law and commandment, crept to the man's feet, whom she neither understood nor controlled, and lavishly poured out her love in a fragrant puddle of oil and salty tears. And they laughed at her. Scorned her. Told her to take her charity to those who needed it. They certainly didn't because they were not the needy poor. They were educated and responsible. They were required to care for the poor, form social justice committees, monitor and castigate the witless for waste, but not humbly receive.

Sitting on this worn red velveteen pew cushion, with the covered buttons wearing to purple, I see the trembling hands of

---

1. Matthew 26:6–11.

a man, soft watery blue eyes staring abstractedly, pat out a prayer on a beloved, borrowed djembe—his surrogate voice. I realize that Jesus was not just being fatalistic. We are not called to fix the poor; we are called to worship with them, talk with them, dream with them, and they with us until *they* become *we*. And when that happens the love that has given them faces will give us eyes, and we will see them and we will reach out our hands, not in charity but with the same love that stoops down twenty times a day and ties a child's shoe.

Of course, it is more complicated than that. I know there is danger and greed and evil to be afraid of. But, like the disciples, we have become enamored with the discourse. We have become comfortable with sorting out the details with our jars of costly ointment neatly shelved for the needy future while the addict on the corner dies without ever having told her story.

But telling her story won't house her or feed her or fix her. It won't make her a "contributor."

Problems need to be fixed. Right?

My arms are so full. My minutes are already spilled out at the feet of my children. And they broke my jar of costly nard two weeks ago "by accident." I close my eyes, letting the dust motes settle on my shoulders, one arm trapping a restless little boy in an embrace of restraint and the other holding a Bible steady as it supports a little girl's artistic embellishment of the bulletin, and I give up making sense of this. I glance the other way at the man wearing bells in his matted beaver-tail hair. I will learn his name. I will learn all of their names, and I will stop asking why it matters.

"Do not despise the poor, because they will be with you always."

Because it is easy to despise what we don't understand. We look at the poor and see them first as problems instead of people. They are the needy and we are those who can supply those needs.

For a year my family worshiped at Haywood Street Congregation, filled with the certain knowledge that it was right to be there, just as a part of the place. We lived in an awkward fluid space, learning and being learned, knowing that it would take time for intentions and practice to become trust and love. A gestation of sorts. We learned names, that there is such a thing as killing cold, that people will hide from help rather than risk losing custody of their child. We learned, there in the womb of that community, that a day of clarity is a praise and a bike is worth blessing. We sat, squirming on the first or second row, sharing joy and sorrows and learning to love.

Then the fluid crystalized into glass and shattered around us. At thirty-eight weeks of gestation, two weeks before her due date, our fourth child slipped from our world to the next. When I felt her stop moving, something stopped moving in me. I was helpless to save her. I couldn't even hold her hand as she faced the great passage from life through death to the great communion of saints. I simply sat and watched her golden curls bounce away across a sunlit mountain meadow and forgot to breathe.

Discharged from the hospital, and wrapped in grief too raw to touch, we found our way back to the red velvet pews. We stood in the congregation as broken as the incontinent addict next to us. Pastor Brian, unable to find words of comfort, acknowledged the power of community and grace and pulled all five of us forward to serve Communion. As I pinched off the tender bread and pressed it into the trembling hands before me, I realized that my hands were trembling too. We had no words, no wisdom, no plan. We were no longer there to serve. Honestly, we were not really there. We stood and sat and sang and hoped that someday we would exist again.

I had become the neighbor at the mercy of the Samaritan's purse. I became the one sitting, broken and bleeding, on the roadside waiting for mercy. At the Communion table there are no "greater callings" or "least of these." We are all simply required to take the bread and know that Jesus is. There in that place, I became real and the poor and needy tended to my hurts. Standing at the front of a congregation of invisible people, tears rolling down my face, I found a kind of peace, a kind of place.

Welcome and Greeting

It was hard and it took time. Because that is what Welcome and Greeting is. It is slow and uncomfortable and the only way that we can truly be. As the triune God called us forth into being in the image of a self in relationship, as our bodies are made of energetic interactions between potential, we can only truly be when we embrace the mystery and awkwardness of the Welcome and Greeting.

Five years ago my family took a trip to lower Alabama. We drove for eight hours in my silver minivan and when we arrived we tumbled into the arms of friends. Deep friends. Friends you would drive eight hours to see. For seven days we gathered around a table together, our children played together, we took care of the tasks of life together, and we talked into the night and chatted under the swings together.

For my husband, Luke, and I, it was a glimpse.

There was a mystical joy happening around the dinner table and in the play corners. We felt something very different during that week lived together. Something rich and beautiful. Something extraordinary and ordinary. Life lived together.

Both of our families are clergy. We do church. We live and breathe the rhythms of the church. We are firmly rooted in the church. But the church was rapidly becoming what was happening out of the corner of our eyes. The squabbles over whom and what we can include within the band of our love and embrace was beginning to scratch the shine right off the dragonfly's back. Our footsteps were beginning to echo ominously in the church halls and we were left feeling like this was not the life we had signed up for.

All the way back to North Carolina, Luke and I talked. We talked about living in community. We had no idea what we were talking about, but heaven and earth had seemed very close in the clutter of joined hearts and lives, and we wanted to snuggle in. We talked about logistics. How could we afford to move into a house large enough to accommodate several families a big as ours? We talked about justice. Doesn't picking who you want to live in community with create an artificial community? Can all people afford to have these conversations, or was this conversation about

CREDULOUS

actualizing our experience of community yet another example of middle-class privilege?

What we were looking for was the true stuff of Welcome and Greeting: relationship and community. The slow community that builds over time and through struggle. I began picking up books about people who had left their fake smiles for something Deep and Profound. People who had packed up or sold everything they had and found the courage to live differently. They called it intentional community. It sounded gorgeous.

I poured over the first three chapters of each of the books, then laid them aside. Something was wrong. My experience and longing were undeniable, but the things I was finding in the books were lofty and exclusive. There didn't seem to be room for me, my children, our dog, gymnastics lessons, and children's choir in these intentional communities.

Many groups dedicated to reimagining communal faith have been gathered under an umbrella of New Monasticism. People who have chosen to step back from the hustle of the predictable flow of life to engage intentionally in a life of contemplation, intention, inclusion, and service. The ideal, packaged and ready to go.

Like many groups, there are markers of who is and who isn't a New Monastic. You, apparently, can't just buy a T-shirt and subscribe to an email list. One of the "Marks" of the New Monastics is moving into neighborhoods of social decline. They call them "abandoned places of Empire."[2]

So we moved into a two-and-a-half-bedroom house with the express purpose of moving to the place we wanted to serve. We had read the books about intentional community, and we wanted to live toward the ethos of New Monasticism. We stood in line for our marks.

It was a great little house, close to the heartbeat of Asheville in a neighborhood that used to be abandoned (now it's the fastest growing neighborhood in our town, so there's that). There was a constant flow of traffic, motorized and pedestrian, in front of our

---

2. Rutba House, *School(s) for Conversion*, 24.

Welcome and Greeting

house. We sat on the porch and gathered around our table and dreamed of the ways that empire could dissolve into community.

Then life began to happen, one baby died and another was on the way. We needed a change of scenery. We wanted another bedroom. The four-bedroom houses are in the suburbs. The suburbs. The minivans of neighborhoods.

I wept real tears. I felt the marks of the New Monastics fading from me like cheap tattoos. But I was tired of living near it all. I couldn't let my kids out to play unattended because I never knew who would be passing by our house and at what speed. Once, our across-the-street neighbor's daughter showed up at my front door to play and all four involved parents panicked because she had crossed the street unattended.

I wanted to live in an abandoned place in the empire, but I moved here, to the suburbs. And I like it here. My kids are safe. I know my neighbors. My kids cross the street all the time without any panic. None. When my toddler goes missing I do not think about kidnapping; I think about muddy pants, I think about falling down stairs, I think about her picking all the neighbor's daffodils.

I am haunted by my comfort. Am I stuck on camelback on the wrong side of a needle? I am haunted by my safety. Am I at risk of being unworthy of Jesus for the sake of my sons and daughters? For months after we moved I looked, lovingly, at the shiny hardwood floors and apologized and rationalized to everyone who would listen for living in such extravagance in the suburbs.

The ideal was moving into the abandon places toward the abandon people, and I had moved to the suburbs on a cul-de-sac.

I always wanted kids. I always wanted four kids. I always want quiet. Somehow it never occurred to me how incompatible those two things are. I think, without having ever done a study or even a thorough survey, the disappointment of having parenthood be mundane and hard is the most shocking part of having kids.

CREDULOUS

"The best moments in my life were the births of my children."
Said every parent ever.
"I am so utterly amazed by how much I love my kids."
Said every parent ever.
"All I want in life is for my kids to be happy."
Said every parent ever.

But, even so, there is a sense of loss, of being overwhelmed, of disappointment. And it feels so wrong.

Kids need so much.
Love.
Help.
Food.
Mercy.
Discipline.

And they don't tire out. Ever. Not even on Sunday afternoon after church.

So, parents get tired and kids keep asking, and, eventually, you find yourself frustrated, isolated, and disappointed. Not all the time. The cliché things are true. You do remember their births, you do love them, you do want the best for them; but life is too much.

So, you fold up your disappointment and hide it away, and you sign them up for gymnastics and violin and kids' yoga and you hope that no one ever finds out how grumpy you are. You hope that no one ever knows that you yelled at your kids today because they screamed "yuck" about another meal. You hope no one ever knows that you pretended that you didn't hear them fighting because you don't have it in you to lecture them one more time about BEING F*&#ING KIND.

And your isolation deepens.

You put on your running tights and quit eating sugar and hydrate, and, still, you feel used up and exhausted. You buy baskets for the crap on the stairs and figure out a chore system and go to the car wash, and, still, you feel like there must be crumbs growing out of the floors. You can't have people over yet. What would they think? We can do community next week—after I clean.

And your isolation deepens.

Welcome and Greeting

Until one day you are sitting on your front porch steps looking at the weeds in the front yard, not-crying. You are not-crying so hard because you are so alone right here in the middle of your family, neighborhood, community, and there is a great mandate in the sky that says you may not show it. You must raise smart, athletic kids, keep a tidy house and bank account, and have the body of a cheetah or leopard—but not a hippopotamus.

The idealism and isolation of parenthood is a place of deep abandonment. It leaves people unable to respond to their own needs and, necessarily, indifferent to the needs of others.

When I first began reading about New Monasticism I had no idea what it was or how it related to me with my clothes-peg gnomes and unit blocks. Monasticism seemed like a serious life of Contemplation and Focus. It seemed like a life stitched to the bias with meaning and mysticism. It seemed like a life decidedly disjunct from mine. New Monastics and I were parallel vectors shot from the same Creative impulse, perhaps, but never intersecting. New Monasticism filled my mind with the ideal embroidered with the unattainable. Patterns of life richly, abundantly intentional all pointing to the depth of meaning that lives lived together can bring.

But I can't do that.

I'm tired.

Like, seriously tired.

Just thinking about crafting my life into something grand and beautiful makes me panicky and weepy.

I think intentional community is fabulous. At least, life with more adults in the house seems attractive. I assume the dishwasher would get emptied and the laundry would get done more often.

But I can't do that.

I can't live in community.

We have four kids and a dog, a snake, three hermit crabs, and two frogs—the hermit crabs are negotiable. We can't just move into a split-level rancher with four other families. Just our shoes take up decades of square feet.

But I can't not.

CREDULOUS

Because something shines through the fancy terms and the heady ideals. Something that sets my heart quivering like harpstrings. Welcome and Greeting isn't a grand life of solemn importance. It is a slow, real life of intention. Somehow, these lines, them and me, they and I, once disjunct, now begin to trend toward each other.

Most of the time, I don't feel like a New Monastic, I feel like a Suburban Monastic. The Divine Office that shapes my life looks more like nap times and snack times than liturgy and prayer, and I have had to make room for the ideal to bubble and spark in the corner while life stumbles forward at the rate of night and morning and calling it good.

And here is the question for this day, New or otherwise: what does it mean to throw your lot in with a new way of living when you have peanut butter on your shirt and one car and seven bicycles in your two-car garage? How do you pour yourself out for others when the lawn may not exceed eight inches in length and the trash needs to be taken to the curb on Tuesday and there are Legos on the floor?

I am not sure that I believe in a preordained, unique calling or plan for each person's life. I know I do not believe that some people are called to lives of depth and service and some are called to more trivial pursuits. I believe that we are all created universally unique. One species making up a population of interconnected, discrete segments. Like a mother and child connected in the womb, we are a species connected through community.

But I do believe in resonance. I don't know why certain things resonate with one person and not another, but I know that there are some things that gather me in and some things that do not. When we returned from our trip to lower Alabama, coated in fairy dust and glistening with ideas, we began to long and to search, and, eventually, we found something new—something that resonated with us down to our bones.

There was a small group of Methodists from Dallas, Texas, who were talking about community. They were a newly forming foundation dedicated to experimenting with different forms of

Christian community, and they hoped for spring in the bleakness of winter. But I had already read those books. I knew where that road led, and there were no vacancies for me.

Paul said so.

Functional belief is what I call those things that drive your behavior that you would argue against over drinks. I functionally believed that since marriage and family brought distraction and worry,[3] since women are told to cover their heads[4] and submit,[5] since Eve exiled us all,[6] it left me, a woman, and especially a mother, out of the good stuff of ministry. My rational mind would argue against this until my tears turned to blood, but I have heard the whisper of "not you" in a place that is deeper than reason. I have deflected the imperative.

I don't believe in the superiority of one person's call over another's, but I functionally believe in it.

So, when Luke was invited to do an intensive training program with the Missional Wisdom Foundation, I was profoundly uninterested. It seemed that these people would be yet another chapter in the same story. Another chorus in the same song. The Unwelcoming Greeting.

Not you.

He began to talk about intentional community. And like anyone does when they feel marginalized, I began to fight and dismiss.

"How is this going to translate for families?"

"If it won't work for us, it won't change mainstream religion."

"What about childcare?"

All the while Paul chattered in the back of my mind. It isn't for you. Not you.

Not for you.

3. 1 Corinthians 7.
4. 1 Corinthians 11:5.
5. Ephesians 5:22.
6. Genesis 3:12.

CREDULOUS

I know you may not be acquainted with my husband, but if you were the next part of my story would not be surprising. After a year of pointedly ignoring his increasingly frequent chatter about community and relationship and the Foundation, I found myself hosting them in my home. They ate with us, we floated the French Broad River with them, and my son fell in love with one of them. And just like that, they became we.

They became we.

Over grills and stoves and campfires, I encountered something I had touched before. Community. Only this time there was no fake smile, no marks of inclusion, and it had taken time. I began to feel the beginnings of a stirring resonance. I talked with them. I laughed with them. And when it came time to cry, I cried with them. Because, truthfully, I fell in love too.

I forgot that they were doing something I couldn't join because I discovered they were doing something I knew how to do. Something I had been practicing for years. They were living into the Welcome and Greeting. It is all part of it—caring for the urban poor, learning names, finding hope. It turns out that the suburbs are places of deep abandonment. Perhaps it is an abandonment dressed in a golf shirt, but there is an ache here. A longing. And if Jesus ate with the lepers, he also ate with the tax collectors—probably in the suburbs.

4

Hymn—Nothing but the Blood

I HAVE HEARD IT said, Methodists love to sing, but I say to you, Methodists love to blend in, and if everyone stands up to sing, by golly, they will stand up and sing too. Whether or not Methodists or Christians love to sing, they do. And hymns are sticky theology. Give the best preacher thirty minutes and he or she might stir your soul, but that closing hymn will dig through your brain for a week.

I began a process of loosening my hold on fundamentalist doctrine while I was in college. Some of the truths that I could accept as a high schooler no longer worked once I became an adult (or one like an adult), and I began to question my truths. Each truth came away like a reluctant scale. It was destabilizing and fragmenting, but the more willing I became to let my doctrines loosen, the freer I became.

I also became more arrogant. As I became more Educated and Enlightened I became caustically critical of what I had been. I created lines of delineation between where I perceived myself to be and where I had been so that I could protect my emerging self. Clearly, I had a raging case of adolescence deep into my twenties.

CREDULOUS

What was anachronistic within this paradigm shift from fundamentalism to post-fundamentalism was that I considered myself to be becoming more inclusive while excluding everything that and everyone who did not echo my set of beliefs. I was angry that I had once been what I could not now be, and I was afraid I would be rejected as inauthentic for having changed. By rejecting my past from a place of fear, I disrupted my connection with everyone but my new tribe. I might not have cared except I discovered that a more expanded view of community could not exist without an acknowledgement of the whole of humanity, even those bits of myself I would rather leave behind.

Since community would not leave me alone and I could not experience true community without finding a way to embrace the whole of who I am and had been, I had to find a way to help who I am now and who I have been hold hands. I found a way of gratitude. If your doctrine makes me into a human porcupine and you are loving people and providing a place for people to connect, I thank God for you. If you read the Bible like a history book and feed the poor, I thank God for you. If you want to walk the Roman road of salvation and you comfort the dying, I thank God for you. There is no way forward into community without true gratitude for all points of view that seek to serve God and love others.

After my baby died, my faith fell apart and deeply theological and philosophical problems seemed uninteresting. God became uninteresting. Why is there suffering? Because life sucks then you die. Why did God not save my baby? Because God isn't. To have no expectation of God? Now, that is a place of freedom. The universe was chaotic and empty. I screamed it to the mountains where the ashes of my baby fed the spring wildflowers. I let it drip down my face as I watched the sun rise, again and again and again.

I insisted that there was nothing, but I could not believe it. I wanted to. I wanted to deny God or spit in God's face, but I could do neither because those flowers were beautiful and the sunrises filled me with wonder.

When I watch my husband baptize a baby, something happens to him. Something changes in his face, usually so practical

Hymn—Nothing but the Blood

and economical, and I can see raw gentleness overtake him. I envy Luke's ordination when I see what baptism does to him.

My second daughter has a gift of embracing. It is an awkward gift for her parents because she will often stop and embrace total strangers. It's awkward for her too. She can feel something well up in her and she is compelled to do something about it. There are times when it is just awkward for everyone, but there are times when the stranger's face will soften, and I know they have received her surprising love.

And there is the dancing sign-turner. Sign-turners are the people who stand for hours at a time and turn the Slow/Stop signs at temporary one-lane-road situations. Luke spent a summer turning a sign during college, so I know how hot, boring, and dangerous the job can be. There is a guy near my house who turns the sign while dancing. For no reason. And I smile when I see him dance. And smiling is good for the soul.

I rejected God the all-powerful because it turned out that God wasn't. All-powerful. I made all the sacrifices, and still my baby died. But, it turns out, there was one whom I could not reject: Jesus. Because Jesus sat down with the rejected and the rejectors and called them by name.

After Peter, who was Simon, caught all the fish on the other side of his boat and wrung his dripping tunic out on the beach, he sat down next to a man with scars. There was a charcoal fire on the beach and fish smoking on sticks.

"Hi." Jesus's grin was lopsided.

"Hi?" Peter's voice had not yet recovered its normal resonance after his swim, but it managed to convey just how inadequate he felt Jesus's word was. A smile was emerging through his panting.

"Fishing good?"

"You know what? Not really. I seem to have lost my knack for it." The smell of the wind shifted the smoke into Peter's face and he waved it away. There had been a charcoal fire in the courtyard that night. The joy and questions that seeing Jesus on the beach had raised, disintegrated in Peter's mind, faded, and blew away with the smoke. "No. Fishing's not really that good today."

"Peter." Jesus tilted his head to try to catch Peter's downturned eyes. His voice was gentle and tinged with laughter. "Do you love me?"

"You know I do." Hadn't they walked together for three years? Hadn't their eyes met over the walked-on water? Hadn't he felt the water on his feet?

"Then feed my sheep." Peter's eyes traced the smoke as it curled around the fish, eyes blistered and mouths stretched wide. He remembered when two fish had fed thousands.

"Peter," Jesus's voice was gentle and low, "do you love me?" His voice carried the hurt of rejection. He set it all in the sand between them. A million, million grains of sand holding up the hurt of three stony rejections.

"Yes, Lord." Peter's voice threatened to crack. He couldn't make his mouth say his name. It seemed disallowed. Not now. Not after he had run.

"Then feed my sheep." Sheep were dirty and the people who fed them were too. The rejects of society. The stories would say that shepherds had been there in the beginning, eager and unashamed of a conquered, displaced, rejected Messiah, and now Jesus wanted a shepherd.

"Peter, do you love me?" This time, Jesus's voice was low but strong. It was a breeze off the desert: hot and welcome. Peter met his eyes.

"Yes." His answer stood. Open and firm. Jesus's face split with a grin and he grabbed Peter's face in both hands and kissed him.

"Then feed my sheep."

In any good story, there is a protagonist and an antagonist. In the story of religion, the religious are often the protagonists and the antagonists, but, that aside, there is a pretty prominent player without whom we could not be called Christians. Christ. A Christian is a follower of Christ.

Hymn—Nothing but the Blood

What is Christ? For me, this is a persistent question.

What is Christ?

Jesus lived two thousand years ago and was called Christ. So, it seems clear that we could infer things about Christ from Jesus.

Who Jesus was and is is the Helen of Troy of questions; it launched a thousand ships and started a war. Sometimes I feel like the most compelling thing about the Christian faith is that people have been willing to fight so hard for their understanding of a thirty-something Jewish man from the first century. Name one Jewish man from the third century. Just one. Name anyone from the third century that wasn't a king or emperor. The most amazing thing about Jesus is that anyone cares who he was.

To engage with who Jesus was and who the Christ was I needed to find a looser approach to life. Jesus the Christ is too thoroughly developed an idea to reimagine from a place of truth. It became important to first rename my truths about Jesus to thoughts. For instance, I changed "Jesus was God incarnate" to "I think Jesus was God incarnate." For me, there is always fear when I loosen a truth to a thought that something cosmic will be harmed in the process. Truth is truth whether or not we truly perceive it, and just because something is believed to be true does not make it truth. The act of loosing my grip on truth has never damaged truth. In my experience it has only allowed it to become bigger, wider, and more beautiful.

Who was Jesus? Jesus spent a lot of time walking, eating, talking, and teaching. Jesus also offered healing and forgiveness to those who came to him. Jesus was a Jewish teacher who lived and preached a message that was so radical that he was, ultimately, killed to try to stop it. History does not give us much more than that.

I have never been to school for theology. No one has ever conferred an ordination on me beyond my baptism. What I am writing here is the stuff of my search and my journey. I invite you in, but I do not intend to convince you. These are my thoughts, not my truths. Please stand if you are able and sing, "Nothing but the Blood" by Robert Lowry.

> What can wash away my sin?
> Nothing but the blood of Jesus;
> What can make me whole again?
> Nothing but the blood of Jesus.

The blood of Jesus. I understand that Lowry was writing about the blood of Jesus on the cross as the atonement for our sin, but I would like to offer another view of the blood of Jesus. The Gospels of Matthew and Luke begin with the bloodline of Jesus. Matthew ties Jesus to Abraham and Judaism and Luke ties Jesus to Adam—thereby tying Jesus to all of humanity. When we speak of incarnation, we speak of the birth of God as a boy, of God becoming flesh, of God implanting into the womb of a woman and, after about nine weeks or so, developing a heartbeat. That is impossible. How can anyone hope to understand the incarnation?

The blood of Jesus—his pulse, his respiration, his living blood—was an expression of the salvific acts of the Divine. Salvation from brokenness, salvation toward wholeness. The incarnation, the enfleshment, the encorporation, made God into someone whose knee bled when he tripped and nose bled when he made his brother too mad. But how is God's blood salvific if it is not dripping from a cross or a doorway?

I believe that when Jesus was born, surrounded by glory and straw, he became a marker for what already was and is and will be. God among us. God with us. God in and through us. Emmanuel. Jesus's blood was not exchanged for guilt through sacrifice. Jesus's blood coursed through his veins as a sign that salvation was possible because God is here with us.

But what will atone for our sin?

Sin. Oh, we love sin. The most egalitarian human trait. All have sinned. And if we have sinned, we need atonement so that we don't go to hell. And Jesus said he was the way the truth and the life, and no one comes to the Father except through him.

Yes.

I remember all of that. How could I forget?

When we read Genesis, the creation myth at the beginning of the Hebrew Scriptures, we read a sweeping story of the creative

Hymn—Nothing but the Blood

force of Love and the nature of God and humankind. There is palpable grace in the lines of these stories. One teller paints a picture of expanses of light and dark, of life bursting forth, of water cascading over the dry stones. Another teller gives shape to the story of us: him, shaped out of the dust, her, brought from his body, and God, together in a garden. There is a rule that is broken, and there is separation. Man from Woman, humans from God, everyone from the Garden.

Whatever separates is sin. Whatever connects is grace.

We know that story.

But what if we told a different story?

What can wash away my sin? What can make me whole again? Nothing but the blood, the life, the incarnation of God.

What is the incarnation of God? Jesus the Christ. The Body of Christ.

In the Gospels we see that Jesus devoted much of his time teaching to creating a new paradigm for the kingdom of God. He kept saying that the kingdom was coming and that many would live to see it come and that is was like very small things. Mustard seeds, yeast, children.

I do not claim to know what Jesus meant, but I think he meant that he, Jesus, was the enfleshed Christ and we can be too. And grace and we are the required elements. Through grace, we, the collective incorporation of Christ, can bring to earth a new kingdom. A way of being in the world that embodies joy and hope and love. Through embodiment of the Christ, the embodiment of love and compassion, any movement toward compassion for self or others is a salvific act of reconnection with the Divine Christ present and working in the world.

What makes us whole is the incarnating Christ.

> Oh! precious is the flow
> That makes me white as snow;
> No other fount I know,
> Nothing but the blood of Jesus.

CREDULOUS

Jesus is, indeed, precious. The flow of his love was overwhelming.

The flow of the love of Jesus is the atomic signature of the Christ. An atomic signature is a unique array of electromagnetic waves or signals that every atom emits and absorbs that allows persons with the right equipment to identify anything on an elemental level. The body of Christ, in all its diversity, is known by love. I do not mean only love given or received in the name of Christ, but love. The love of the Jew, the Greek, the Muslim, the agnostic, the addict, the sex worker, the evangelical, or the pope is the signature of the living Christ, incarnate in us, come again.

Jesus was sitting on a stone, his head aching from the glare of the sun and the dust of the dry Judean countryside. The Pharisees were finally done questioning him. Andrew laid a hand on his shoulder. Andrew always noticed when his head had begun to ache.

"Master, rest here. I'll go get you a drink."

"Make it a strong one." Jesus shook his head and rubbed the back of his neck. "I'm tired of fighting."

"I know you are." Andrew walked away, calling to one of the others to fetch him a wineskin.

It had been a terrible day. The dust coated his hands and feet and hair and voice. The sun and the questions had pried into every crevice. He was simply spent. He felt like a grape pressed flat and left in the sun. He sagged against the rock and ran his fingers through his hair. The Pharisees wanted to know if a man could divorce his wife. They wanted to know how far their obligation went. He pinched the bridge of his nose. *Yes*, he sighed, *the law says you can divorce your wife and leave her defenseless, but should you? These women, these children, who would speak for them? Who would care for them?*

Hymn—Nothing but the Blood

Jesus noticed a woman approaching. She was also tired. Her clothes were wrinkled and smudged from the accumulated tugs of her brood of children. There were four of them. All small. One had a thumb stuck in her mouth. The mother pushed the tallest toward Jesus, determined to reach this teacher that everyone had been whispering about. A teacher who had women speaking for him. The child stumbled exactly two steps forward then froze, staring at the dirt.

"Come here, friend," Jesus said, patting the rock next to him.

He met the mother's eyes. He saw the miles she had walked from her home. He saw the weight of the youngest child in her arms. He saw the strength of this woman.

She had come, knowing she would have to walk back to her home, exhausted, to meet her equally exhausted husband. He would be hungry and she would have to revive the fire and mix the flour with the oil she had pressed from the few olives from their scraggly olive tree. She also knew she would smile as she told her husband of this moment.

"May I hold the baby for you?" Jesus stretched his arms up. The baby's eyes widened and she turned her head in fear as the mother dropped her weight into the arms of the teacher. Jesus noticed a braid of purple thread around the baby's wrist. "What's your name, little one?" The baby held herself stiffly away from him for a moment, then, sensing her mother was not going away, relaxed.

"Her name is Deborah," the woman said shaking out her arms. "Please, sir, we have come a long way. Will you bless my children?"

He could see Andrew hurrying back with concern plastered all over his face. Jesus lifted a hand to wave him off. There was time. There would always be time for children.

Yes, precious is the flow of this love.

> For my pardon, this I see,
> Nothing but the blood of Jesus;
> For my cleansing this my plea,

CREDULOUS

Nothing but the blood of Jesus.

Yes, but what about sin? What about evil? What about suffering?

I know.
I have suffered. I have caused suffering. I know that suffering is real. I don't know why there is injustice or pain or sorrow or hurt or anger or aggression. I don't know.
I do not say that the Christ is love from a place of perfection. I claim that Jesus, the Christ, has made me whole despite my brokenness. Yes, there is evil in the world. Yes, people, even people who claim to be followers of Jesus, project the anti-Christ into the world. I admit my part in this. I have been narrow. I have been envious. I have not loved my neighbor. I have refused to hear the cry of the needy. I have refused to hope.
Forgive me.

> Nothing can for sin atone,
> Nothing but the blood of Jesus;
> Naught of good that I have done,
> Nothing but the blood of Jesus.

If Paul was a Jew among Jews, I am a firstborn among firstborns. I live my life religiously. About twenty years ago, I went hiking in the Blue Ridge Mountains of western North Carolina with my family and some family friends. The place where we were hiking crossed a rocky bald where there were patches of sensitive lichen. A helpful sign instructed hikers to follow a trail of yellow painted dots to minimize the ecological impact of hundreds of booted feet. After a few minutes of ambulatory dot-to-dot, we sat down to look at the view. My mother, always aware of her children, had seen my careful attempts to minimize my lichen impact, and teasingly asked if I was sitting on a dot.

I was sitting on two.

Hymn—Nothing but the Blood

I have done quite a bit of good. But to what purpose? Somehow, we, the church, are still living balanced on a scale with our ancient Egyptian friends. Am I good or am I evil? Yes.

I am good and I am evil.

As I journey through the Christian experience, life, struggle, I have come to believe strongly in grace. It seems like an intangible dimension in which we move. It is present in our motions of goodness and not annihilated by our motions of evil. I do not understand its nature, but I have felt it. It could be atonement, but it does not have to be.

John Wesley taught about the different natures of grace. He taught that baptism was a way for people to receive grace. Baptism is a moment and a motion. A moment of naming this one as a child of God and a motion of ongoing work. Yes, there might be a moment of justification—atonement—but the funny thing about moments is that we don't get the whole picture.

Einstein's theories involving space and time have shown (to other people) that space and time converge in some way, and, somehow, that shakes out to mean that, from the standpoint of physics, all time is now.

I have really tried to grasp this. I have. Maybe someday I will. Within this theory, I already have. Even though now-me doesn't truly understand them, Einstein's theories give a definite nuance to our experience of time. Even though we experience time in a linear way, it is not the most accurate understanding of time, but, because we cannot experience time in its fullest sense, we are left feeling like our experience of time is paramount.

If all time and space are concurrent, how can we speak of a moment of atonement? If all time is now, then you exist in all forms of yourself, now. Our only response to that, other than puzzlement, must be this: life is contained in the infinity of now. There is no before or after; there is simply going further into now. Now is the intersection of grace and the Christ. Now is the joining of the self and the anti-self. If you choose to become present to now, folding into the flow of love, then the infinity of now will become the abundant, eternal life all were promised.

CREDULOUS

Since I cannot grasp the infinite nature of a moment, confined, as I am, to a linear experience of time, I must satisfy myself with this: life is more complex than our doctrines can explain and the courage to be now, to be here, seems very important.

> This is all my hope and peace,
> Nothing but the blood of Jesus;
> This is all my righteousness,
> Nothing but the blood of Jesus.

Finding yourself swept up into the incarnational love of the Divine requires equal parts intention and release.

In silence and acknowledgement of who and where I am, I gather the courage for action. Hope and peace. There is fear in this. Losing yourself feels terrifying. Sometimes I don't. Sometimes I march out in the fullness of my own incarnation. Sometimes I act as my own anti-self. I acknowledge that. Yes, that too is me. But so is the blood and life of Jesus. When I lost my baby I walked away from faith. No, I stomped away. I sat down on the path of my life, ready to spend at least the infinity of several moments parked. I had no interest in anyone's incarnation except the failed incarnation of my child. In a way, I am still there. I acknowledge that.

This hope and peace pulls us into life both of strength and weakness. We are compelled into stillness and action.

> Now by this I'll overcome—
> Nothing but the blood of Jesus,
> Now by this I'll reach my home—
> Nothing but the blood of Jesus.

I just spent three hours cleaning up the room shared by my second and third children. I begged, threatened, and cajoled my children to help me. I lost my temper when I found a basket of washed, dried, and folded clothes carelessly upended onto the floor. Every time I clean up my home, I am filled with grating antipathy for the world of physical science. Could we not have been dropped into a universe that tended toward order?

But we haven't been. We have been dropped into a world that tends towards chaos.

Hymn—Nothing but the Blood

Poverty is chaos.
Racism is chaos.
Loss is chaos.
Brutality is chaos.
An ocean full of plastic is chaos.

Our world tends toward chaos, and Jesus, a man who lived in this universe according it its laws, left this commission: train disciples, bringing order to a world bent on chaos through the power of Trinitarian baptism.[1]

It is not our commission to save people from eternal torment. It is our commission, those who desire to follow Jesus in his life as the Christ, to bring attention to chaos, and it is through the power of the incarnate Christ that the laws of nature can be reversed. This is the story of resurrection. Through the power of the ongoing incarnation of Christ, the laws of the universe, which tend toward disorder, can be reversed through resurrection.

This is truly good news. We are not powerless against the tide of entropy. We are resurrected through love. The chaos that threatens to tear the fabric of who we are and who we want to be is quieted through the mystical inpouring of grace from the Divine. We are loved. We are seen.

In a world where the incarnate Christ overcomes chaos,
Poverty is seen.
Racism is seen.
Loss is seen.
Brutality is seen.
An ocean full of plastic is seen.

And when chaos is seen by love, it loses its power. When a hand reaches out to wash another's foot, when a coat is wrapped around a cold body, when privilege stands between the aggressor and the marginalized in peace and strength, then chaos loses its power. It is through the incarnation of the Christ through those who swing their intention toward the life of the Divine that humanity can find hope to overcome hate and evil.

---

1. Matthew 28:16–20.

CREDULOUS

> Glory! Glory! This I sing—
> Nothing but the blood of Jesus,
> All my praise for this I bring—
> Nothing but the blood of Jesus.

In a world that has lost its focus on organized religion, what relevance does the body of Christ have? What hope does the church, of any flavor, offer? What does faith extend to a world with a mandate toward chaos?

Nothing.

Nothing that is not already there. Grace pools at our feet whether or not we have eyes to see it. This is the infinite glory of the Divine. The life of faith simply offers this: develop eyes to see the grace and the chaos. For there is no way to begin to see the grace without also seeing the chaos. What does the incarnation of the Christ ask from you?

> To acknowledge your humanity.
> To acknowledge the humanity of the other.

Religion as an institution is no longer necessary. The smartphone is now the opiate for the masses. The church and its god are dead or dying. The life of Jesus calls to us to take up the cross of our sorrow, our hopelessness, our apathy and take one step toward stillness, one step toward love, one step toward incarnation.

This, then, is the resurrection and the life.

5

Creed

Is there any need to rope off our beliefs? Do the creeds serve any purpose other than taxonomical? If I am to have the courage to place my feet into the footprints of Jesus, and so continue the work of the Christ in the world, I do not need to know what size his feet were. I simply need to stand up and walk.

Luke's final project with the Missional Wisdom Foundation's program on beginning and leading intentional communities was to begin and lead an intentional community. I was annoyed.

At the time we were attending three worship services a week with small children, and he wanted to try a house church. It seemed cumbersome and redundant. I didn't want to add anything else to my life.

Our first task as a house church was to study and craft a Rule of Life. A rule of life is a set of guidelines around which one volunteers to form her life. We, eleven adults and ten children, gathered and ate a potluck supper then sat and discussed a rule of life. There was a sample in the book we were using[1] and we were more than willing to discuss it. The sample was broken into five parts and

---

1. Heath and Kisker, *Longing for Spring*, 52.

we dutifully, methodically broke it into five weeks, reading the correlative parts before meeting. We took turns watching the kids plummet down the driveway on wheels and sitting on the couch engaged in spirited intellection about a sample rule of life.

But the sample rule of life never matured into a Rule of Life. We said we would try the sample for a while. We thought we could ease our way in. But we were too polite to ask for commitment.

But something within me longed for a dotted line to sign.

I wanted an anchor.

Because that was the fall that our daughter died. It was like standing on a parapet on the fourth floor of a sand castle and watching the tide roll in. The sand walls began to slump in and the beautifully crafted walls surrounding my faith correlatively lost their form. The creeds, the gems of my childhood, so carefully memorized and protected, faded to gravel. Cynicism and anger broke down their beauty and all I could see was patriarchy and control.

For a while I tried to rebuild my walls. It was an effort of sandbags and drip castles—but the magic was gone.

When the tide swept back, there was nothing left but smooth sand and a little sea foam.

I left footprints as I walked away.

In the midst of grief I remember bruising myself and my husband as waves of rage coursed through my body like demons. There is no way to recover tidily from trauma of that magnitude. Grief changes everything.

Grief. My blank slate.

I found comfort in the mantle of atheism. I took up disbelief like a blanket laced with Novocain. Life didn't hurt so much if I denied the existence of God. No one forgot to guide my baby safely to the shores of the mortal world. No one saw the darkness in my heart and withdrew his protection. No one orchestrated the death of my baby to harvest a cosmic silver-cloud lining. Because there was no One. The I AM became the I AM NOT.

I wanted to reframe my world. I wanted to eliminate my construct of God, which was no longer comforting. I wanted to. I pleaded with myself, with my husband (who didn't fight me), with the wind itself, until my rage was exhausted, and I was left with dissatisfaction. I might be unwilling to allow for a God who drowned the world in a fit of cosmic frustration, but there were things about my experience that amounted to an image of something unseen and unknown. Why is it that some music makes me cry? Why are people compassionate?

I am sure that, if you dig far enough, most kindness could be traced to a kind of self-preservation. Periodically my children are on probation from screen time until I "see a marked improvement in [their] kindness toward each other." During those times my boys shower each other with acceptance and love while, over the other one's shoulder, giving me the "Is this good enough?" eye. Sometimes kindness springs from self-love, but it seems to me that compassion comes from a different place. It seems that compassion taps into who we are at our best.

Kindness might compel me to bring cans to a food drive, but compassion would give me the courage to look the hungry in the eye and acknowledge our commonality. Kindness might remind me to deliver Christmas cookies to my neighbors, but compassion gives me the courage to let my neighbor see me cry. Kindness might help me to pray for someone; compassion gives me the courage to sit with a person while they suffer. And I have done those things and I have seen them done. And I am just credulous enough to believe there might be a reason why.

So, I have a problem. I am caught, unwillingly, between belief and unbelief. My journey hasn't been neat. It has been a wandering way. I can't form God into sentences much less a creed. I can only find images and silence, despair and laughter.

One night, at one in the morning, with tears running down my face and soaking into the neck of my T-shirt, I wrote my first apophatic essay. Technically, it was an apophatic ultimatum. Apophatic statements assert what God is not. I was wrestling with the story of Noah for obvious reasons, and I found that I would rather not believe in God than believe in a God who would kill every living thing on earth except a select few just because that God was angry and disappointed. Because if we are to call this being Heavenly Father, I would rather not believe he has a homicidal rage problem.

I asserted that if I was going to believe in God, if any value remained in a system of belief—which I doubted thoroughly—God must not be vengeful, male, or elsewhere. That was all I could face. I had heard it said that I had been created in the image of this God, but I say to you, I could only see the familial defects. Anger, disappointment, jealousy: I could see those things in the image of God I bore. But that statement of belief could not bring me hope. It could not bring me joy. So I turned to what was mystery.

Negative space is the image that is created by what is not. When the vision of my soul is blurred with tears or anger, I find that affirmations of belief seem hollow and constraining. If depression has tinged everything with skepticism, then doctrinal assertions become thin and spongy. Flavorless and unappealing. When I cannot summon the courage to affirm what God is, or even that God is, I turn to inhabiting the negative space.

> God is not hatred.
> God is not vengeful.
> God is not arbitrary.
> God is not exclusive.
> God is not hurtful.

The thing about wide spaces is you can see the entire arc of the rainbow. I might hate that the story of Noah has been used to punish and threaten, but, even knowing that a rainbow is light refracted through water droplets, I still stop when I see one painted through the sky. And the funny thing is, even though I have my a-Theist file folder bulging with proof that there can't possibly be a God, I can't stop believing in a Creator. God as Creator fills me with drive and purpose, and gives my identity power. Because I am a creator. I have brought forth life from my body. My body broke and healed to give life to my children. I wake up every morning faced with the task of bringing my mental chaos and theirs to order. I am tasked with shedding light on what is darkness, and guiding these hearts toward love and compassion. What does the negative space teach me about God?

God is love.
God is forgiving.
God is purposeful.
God is inclusive.
God is healing.

When Jesus walked the dusty streets of Israel in the year 30 or so, he depended on the hospitality of his friends and followers. We don't hear any stories about him returning to his home, so often Jesus is counted among the homeless. Jesus preached a very strange message. He spoke of the blessedness of the broken. The heroes of his stories were the outcasts who showed compassion on those dying in the ditches. He loved those no one else even saw and admonished his followers to do the same.

Feed the hungry. Clothe the naked. Tend the sick.

Jesus's words echo in my ears as I pinball around my house, chasing the wreckage that kids can create, and I often wonder how the work of *my* hands can be counted in the kingdom of God.

I know there are those who suffer hunger and cold within the limits of my city, but I am so mired down in laundry, meals, and runny noses that I cannot imagine incorporating one more mission into my day much less leaving the house.

If you love me, feed my sheep.

But, of course, I can't, and the guilt puddles in the corner next to the plastic toy hammer and a hardened ball of orange and vermillion Play-Doh. I know that this man, the incarnation of God, embodying the Christ and asking us to embody the Christ, has told Martha that her work was not valuable. I have always been a willing disciple. I will gladly drop down at the knee of a favorite and listen. Mary and I would spend our time angling for the best patellar perch.

Except for the needs of my children. Of which the kingdom of God is made.

Jesus came to bring a kingdom different from the kingdoms of the world. It is not a city of heroes. In a society focused on achievement and superlative, the invisible life of a mother can seem insignificant. In a spirituality focused on service to the marginalized and contemplation of the Divine, what I can muster—donating clothes, teaching my sons that stop means stop, and noticing that creation is inimitably moving—seems insignificant.

Whether or not we are on good terms with or even know our mothers, we cannot escape having one. No one comes to the Father except through the womb of a mother, but often our mothers are treated like the Eves of our lives. Scapegoats responsible for our tics and insecurities—and sometimes they are. We are all born wanting to know if we can ever live without them. Our lives are too entwined. We rebel and fling out our tiny wills, flailing against the knowledge that we did not birth ourselves.

Even Jesus struggled with his mother. And maybe that is my statement of faith about Jesus. Jesus, God incarnate, struggled. He was awkward, dismissive, and sarcastic. But, when the crowds were there, hungry, and he was in great need of a Martha, he fed them with great compassion.

While I wrestle with what it means to be "mother," I am content knowing I am where I am supposed to be. I spend every moment of my life feeding, clothing, and tending the hungry, naked, and distressed. For this moment, it is enough. While I may someday move out of these walls, for now, I am here.

After all, Jesus rolled the grain when his disciples were hungry. Jesus answered questions again and again and again. Jesus touched the dirty and the sick. Jesus was awake when everyone else slept.

Jesus was a mother.

Creed

Holy Fire, Mystery,
Before the world began you were there, unseen, moving, creating. Hovering like a hen, wings outspread over her chicks, you brushed the face of creation in a caress of delight and love and it still feels the warmth of your touch. In shimmering moments and hidden corners, the Spirit-joy of creation spills out.

A river begins as a spring, and is pulled, by gravity, downhill, never completely satisfied until it has dropped its contents into the wide expanse of the ocean. Where does the road begin? Has it ever occurred to you that every road on any given landmass is just part of one long winding path with about a billion dead ends? We are all connected by the pathways under our feet.

Where does the spirit begin? The ancient creeds minutely describe our beliefs about the Son and his life, death, and resurrection, but the Spirit, mystical and ineffable, cannot be described.

We believe in the Holy Spirit.

We often cannot muster up more than that. A subject and a verb and a prepositional phrase with an article and an adjective. We believe. Like the wind or the dawn or fireflies, we are intimately familiar with it, but we can no more explain it than we can produce it. This thing scares us, and, in our unease, we seek to control and circumscribe it. We invoke it with songs and raised hands, but if it shows up we are terrified of what could happen. We are weary and worn and we seek refreshment, but the Spirit does not bring just refreshment. We are met with mystery when what we searched for was clarity. We are handed a wraith when we wanted a letter. Give us something to read, to hold, to use, but not the wind.

Not this gentle, terrifying generality.

God can't be general because God is mine, my own, my precious.

CREDULOUS

The Christian story is a story of failure. Adam and Eve, distrusting God's love, chose to take matters into their own hands. Abraham, distrusting God's promise, used a woman and discarded her. Peter, distrusting God's means, denied his closest friend. This is Christ's holy church. A cloud of witnesses. Or defendants.

The curtain tore, the Word made flesh was made Word, and the Spirit found a terrified group of deserters in a locked church, holding a closed worship service, mourning their private loss. The breath that had rippled the primordial waters and filled a valley of dry bones with dancing shook the locks off the doors and the defendants became witnesses.

This Spirit, this Mystery, does not belong to us.

In the beginning God created the heavens and the earth and the Spirit hovered over the waters. Dark and chaotic. The Spirit is not afraid of our chaos. Spirit was not meant to be ordered and tidy. Spirit is creative and risky. In the intersection of water and wind, we find truth. We are not assured of wealth, power, or riches; we are assured of grace, mercy, and justice. We are not assured of happiness; we are assured of abundance.

The Spirit of God is indescribable. A universal truth only seen out of the corner of your mind. A vapor too ephemeral to grasp, but a power that sets the world dancing and whispers the soul-prayers of us all to the Creator.

6

Anthem—Sing Me to Heaven

THE CHOIR IS SINGING one of my favorite anthems, "Sing Me to Heaven," by Daniel Gawthrop. It is a piece of poetry written to be sung. It is music written for poetry. Its lines are economical and expansive. And the choir is singing it without me.

I have sung in choirs my whole life, and I have never sung it.

I first heard "Sing Me to Heaven" when I was twelve years old. I was in the children's choir, and the chamber choir, for which I was never brave enough to audition, sang it from the balcony. I was transfixed. Later, the Furman Singers, my alma mater's prestigious voice-major choir, sang it. I was in the women's chorale—for piano majors (which I was). Now my church's choir is singing it. I used to sing with them, but then my kids aged out of nursery. Now I sit in the pew with my kids, singing along softly, tears leaking from the corners of my eyes. For me, this music manifests the ideal. An ideal that haunts me Divinely.

The ideal is the measure of our best possibility. It is sitting by a clear rock-bottom river with the rhododendron in full bloom with birds riffing treble over the water's base notes. But sometimes

CREDULOUS

you are at home and there are crumbs on the couch and the dog is snoring and there is peanut butter and a creepy doll on the counter.

I am not a perfectionist.

I am not a perfectionist, and it kills me because I crave perfection, but I don't have the drive to make perfection happen. At the end of the day, the unfolded laundry that sat all day on my bed, waiting to be perfectly quartered and patted into its drawers, will get returned to the baskets on the floor because I lack the will of a perfectionist.

But, the next day I will dump it all back on the bed knowing that this day will be different. I will fold all the clothes, I will put them all away, I will button the top button of all the hang-ups, I will probably have time to iron the little cotton dresses, and it will all be done before bedtime.

I am an idealist.

I am an idealist, and it kills me because nothing is ever ideal. Even if I manage to get the laundry folded, someone will dump their basket looking for their favorite underpants.

I used to be the music director at a church. Part of my responsibilities included organizing and directing the adult church choir. If you have ever been to a mainline Protestant church service that tends toward the traditional, you will have seen an adult church choir. Usually about half way through the service, the adult church choir will stand up in front of the congregation and sing a song that, ideally, correlates with the scripture around which the service, ideally, centers. This is generally called the anthem, which comes from the word *antiphon*, which means to sing something back and forth. It is rare that the anthem is antiphonal.

As I dug through the sheet music, tidily cataloged in wall-to-wall metal file cabinets, I read the anthem titles and thought about the way that, once enfleshed through corporate singing, they would lift the gathered community to engage meaningfully with the text and provide the space of spiritual resonance that some can only find through music.

Anthem—Sing Me to Heaven

I picked hymns based on the texts, not the tunes. I was proud of how meticulously I combed though the texts to pick something that would reflect the scripture of the day. During high holy seasons like Lent, I would pick hymns regardless of their singability or familiarity to make sure that the ideal stage was set for worship. It is shocking how annoyed people get when they have to sing something they don't know in public.

My particular adult church choir was full of the grace and wisdom that comes with age. Also, some of the deafness. *If you have never engaged in group singing, it might be important to know, for the purposes of this story, that in choral singing hearing is usually an asset.* I remember one evening, when I was doing announcements during Wednesday night adult church choir rehearsal, one of the gentlemen asked me to "speak up" because he "couldn't hear." He had his hand cupped around his ear and everything.

I remember standing there, in the full flower of my youth and third pregnancy, agreeing to speak as loudly as I could while freaking out in my mind. How was I supposed to fulfill the expectations of centuries of choral tradition and elevate the souls of the congregation with singers who couldn't hear? My planning involved textual themes and harmonic resonance, not hearing impairment. I was there to stir the souls of the gathered community toward contemplation and wonder. We were, after all, leading Worship.

I have always longed for the ideal. The ideal has always been elusive.

I homeschool my four children. In my own home. I really should find someone else's home to use because it pretty much destroys my house every single day. I was raised as a homeschooler from first through twelfth grade. I am not sure I ever seriously considered not homeschooling. Somewhere between my memories of playing in woods filled with dry leaves and adolescent mornings wrapped up in the words of gothic novels, I developed my definition of ideal childhood. It seemed a very abundant life, and my husband and I decided that it was a life we wanted for our children.

But it is hard.

CREDULOUS

Homeschooling brings me to my knees regularly. It never quite turns out how I pictured. I suppose there are moments that do, but the preponderance of the time is spent untangling who stole who's pencil or pen or rubber band or toast or socks. It is very sophisticated and glamorous.

I think I began homeschooling when my eldest son was four months old. That was when we started our first music class. There were four in the class. Two of us were moms. When we began the class, both infants were just learning to roll over and by the time we finished, they were crawling. The teacher told us the Really Important Reasons that early childhood music is important, and I listened. I was ready. In fact, I got certified in Early Childhood Music. I was so ready.

The ideal lured me forward. I dreamed of planting gardens while explaining pollination and the water cycle to my eager learners. I wanted to make the perfect space, the ideal space. I dreamed of a room filled with wooden manipulatives and maps. I hoarded pictures of gorgeous ateliers and began collecting vintage clothespins for Waldorf-style gnomes. I collected sensory material. I worried that I didn't have a Montessori food-prep station. And I dreamed of words. Buckets of words. Words we would read, words we would sing, words we would recite. Beautiful, meaningful words.

I remember sitting on the floor in my son's room when he was about seven months old, fretting because I hadn't managed to teach him his colors. Yet.

"This block is blue. Can you touch the other blue block?

"That block is green. Can you touch the blue block? Which one is blue?

"Which one is blue?

"Can you point to the blue one?

"Blue. Blue?"

The ideal finds a way to distract from the beauty of the mundane. The mundane is what happens when our dreams meet

Anthem—Sing Me to Heaven

reality. I live with a picture of ideal homeschooling, ideal relationships, and the ideal home cluttering up my experience of what is real. There always seems to be something tantalizingly exciting scooting along in front of me. It keeps me motivated. It gives me the energy to write a book in the middle of raising four kids. It drives me to look for better ways to order my time so that I can make all my minutes count. But, it tends to cloud the daily motions of my life with a fine mist of disappointment.

Raising kids, doing ministry, writing books—these things are supposed to be a long stream of meaningful and satisfying intentional interactions. I have imagined peaceful picnics under ancient maple trees with children dressed in tidy, coordinating outfits. Our conversation ebbs and flows between storytelling and mirth. We are all happy to be where and with whom we are. Periodically natures intrudes in gentle, non-stinging, and educational ways. Eventually, after the children have happily eaten everything on their plates with praise and thanksgiving on their lips, they scamper off to fly kites or climb trees or build fairy houses out of acorns.

The disappointment of finding out that life is mostly waiting and preparing for something that turns out to be about half as satisfying as you hoped can obliterate the small, mundane beauties of fairy houses made out of uneaten raisins. The ideal is what gets me out of bed in the morning, but the real, the mundane, the actual, keeps me out of bed.

With ten thousand footprints in yesterday's snow and the clamor of my kids reenacting a drastically modified version of *Henry V* drifting up from below, I now appreciate that life happens slowly. Everyone says kids grow up fast, and they do—in retrospect—but the moment-to-moment is slow, and every moment is valuable even if nothing is crammed into it and the space is not perfect. They learn their colors. They can cook in the kitchen. All the words seep in. It all happens so slowly. It all happens so quickly—life unfolds at the pace of a day, one inexorable revolution at a time.

It is when the mundane breaks through the ideal that I discover that grace was there all along. Dew drops glisten and soak your shoes. Children laugh and bicker. Your photograph never captures the glory of the sunset, but you try anyway. The mundane blossoms into glory when we release it from the tyranny of idealism.

And faith is no different.

In the Methodist tradition there are two official sacraments: eucharist and baptism. Eucharist is the gathering of the community of faith and the community of saints around the table in remembrance of Jesus the Christ—emptying oneself for the other and allowing the whole of creation to minister to one's needs. Baptism is when water is used to symbolize the death and resurrection or rebirth of a person into the kingdom of God. A sacred bath of grace. Both sacraments are enacted by God through the medium of grace. Both take place in community. Both have been plagued by idealism throughout the Christian narrative.

As I sit in the pew one Sunday morning, helping my five-year-old conduct the anthem (he's pretty good—he has a terrific sense of timing and line), it occurs to me that I have put off claiming my place in God's kingdom because I am waiting for the ideal to materialize. I am faced with a liminal space. The space between the mundane and the ideal. If I wait for the ideal time, knowledge, or invitation, I will wait forever.

Here in this place where people have gathered for generations, waving my arms in tandem with my son in silent communion with these words, so beloved and so ideal, the "Not yet"s, "Not you"s, and "Not now"s seem muffled. I, in the desperate hopefulness of singing, decide that I want to live into *and* instead of *or*. I want to live in a world where the mundane and the ideal hold hands. I want to acknowledge that life is an abundance of the ideal and the mundane, and this, this *and*, is the message of grace. The message of grace is, "Yes, you. Yes, now."

Perhaps that is why on Jesus's last night with his disciples he washed their feet and taught them to eat in remembrance of the gospel. Through the act of washing and eating, Jesus made the mundane holy.

7

Prayer of the People

WHEN IT COMES TO prayer, I will admit, right up front, I struggle.
I struggle with the forms, the purpose, and the results of prayer.

Our Father, who art in heaven, hallowed be thy name. Thy kingdom come, thy will be done, on earth as it is in heaven. Give us this day our daily bread, and forgive us our debts as we forgive our debtors. And lead us not into temptation, but deliver us from evil. For thine is the kingdom and the power and glory forever. Amen

I remember praying. In college I knelt in a sanctuary not too far from where I live now, pouring myself out on behalf of anything that caught my attention. That was intercessory prayer. I knew, deeply, that my prayer could and did move the Spirit of God to act on the behalf of those for whom I prayed. I also remember driving to church on Sunday morning believing that if I could spend that time in constant prayer, then I would get all green lights. That was not intercessory prayer. That was interstate prayer. I remember praying to fall asleep and praying that food I left on the counter all night wouldn't give me food poisoning and praying for self-control.

But, throughout all this prayer, something felt unsettled about prayer. Unsettling. I got green lights, but on Sunday morning when driving with the usual flow of traffic that is probably not supernatural. In the back of my rational mind I knew that. I knew that God didn't turn the lights green because God loved me and wanted me to get to church on time—even if I left a few minutes late. After all, a green light for me meant a red light for someone else.

Then my husband went to divinity school and he learned all about the history and theology behind our prayers. So, I began to pray as Jesus taught us. I began to pray as the church taught us. I didn't want to get swept up into the magical thinking of my past, so I decided to stick to the tradition of the church. But, predictably, I began to feel detached from prayer. Prayer became professional. And that was awkward.

When I am sitting in church listening to someone pray—eloquently—for a long time, I feel like a spectator, at best, or, at worst, a voyeur. Not only is keeping children quietly respectful for the eternal minutes of the well-crafted prayer rather rigorous from a parenting standpoint, listening to someone pray is strange. I know the intent is for the congregation to "join their hearts" with the pray-er, but it seems like the real invitation is to enter into awe and wonder at the profundity of the words and the smoothness of the elocution.

I obviously have a deep degree of brokenness in my relationship to prayer. I carry a sense of resentment and skepticism into any prayer practice or event. I am suspicious this is because there is something too important to abandon to the wayside here. There are so many things that I have easily laid aside: praise music, biblical literalism, gendered language for God—but prayer and I are at an impasse. I want to be an a-pray-ist. But, like my stint with atheism, I am unsatisfied with that.

I have prayed for healing, for miracles, for help, for guidance for myself and for others, and I have or have not been answered. I

Prayer of the People

stopped telling people I was going to pray for them because I could never remember to do it. Not from laziness or forgetfulness but, rather, from a frustration with or confusion about what prayer is. I carry a considerable amount of guilt about my inability to pray well for people. I don't really know where I am with prayer. At the very least, I don't believe there is a transactional nature to prayer.

I told you. I struggle.

After the death of my daughter I consciously did not pray. I could not shake the feeling that if I believed in prayer and I hadn't prayed diligently for my daughter's safe arrival, which I hadn't, her death was partially my fault. A murder by omission. Truthfully, it didn't cross my mind to pray that my baby would be born safe. I thought God would understand that implicitly. After all, God is a parent, right? When I leave my children with my mother, I do not feel it necessary between the "here are the diapers" and "this is bedtime" instructions to include a "please do not let them die" instruction.

I probably don't need a psychoanalyst to help me parse out where my struggle with prayer comes from.

But there was a time when I believed in prayer.

There was a time when people whom I didn't know would lean over in church and ask me to pray for them.

There was a time when I would offer to pray for a group meal.

But not now. Not now when I can't even figure out how to begin. Because somewhere along the way, *Dear Heavenly Father* stopped making sense. It does not agree with my current understanding of God. As I lean more deeply into the center of who I think God might be, a salutation seems awkward. When I close my eyes and think about God, I do not think of a male figure who is away in heaven. I believe God is here.

55

CREDULOUS

God is here.
God is.
God.

God is not the fabric of life.	God is here.
God is not the threads that are woven into the fabric of life.	God is.
God is the twist that holds the fibers of the threads of life together.	God.
God is not the air we breathe.	God is here.
God is not the oxygen that fuels the fires in our cells.	God is.
God is the dance of the electrons and the mystery of the nucleus.	God.

Dear genderless, unanthropomorphized, incomprehensible force or being or reality or background (not somewhere in the sky, but, apparently, needing to be addressed as if unaware of my intention or attention or need).

See, that seems awkward.

I have not reconciled myself to prayer. Do I not understand, or is there nothing to understand? Reason and logic can't reassure me about prayer, but I have a deep feeling that I should sit with it for a bit longer. I almost don't want to, but I will try. It is, after all, listed right there after "Anthem."

I was taught to pray. I know how. I know that prayer is supposed to be listening to as well as talking to God. I know that there are types like intercessory, centering, and congregational. And I know that I don't know. I was taught that when we pray we should

Prayer of the People

begin by praising God. It is tempting for me to become more cynical here and mention that beginning with flattery seems to be a good idea with despots and gods alike, but I won't because I have also been taught that God doesn't need to be praised; humans need to praise God.

Today, with the sunlight creating window-blind stripes on the carpet and my children playing peacefully in the other room, I feel a sort of privileged guilt about praising God. Right now, I am exceedingly comfortable. Right now, my children are healthy and well. Right now, the sky is clear blue, the air is breathable, and polar bears are not extinct.

God, you are the provider of my needs. God, you are the protector of my children. God, your creation is whole and good.

But these phrases are not what my deep heart is crying out. This is not where my true prayer begins. I am angry. I am afraid. I am tired.

God, the poor have sores on their hands from the cold. God, the addicted frighten themselves and others. God, the air is filling with poisons.

God. God! God?

Ok, let's keep going. Next, we are supposed to express gratitude. This is a good idea. Gratitude has all kinds of provable positive effects on the grateful, so it couldn't hurt.

Thank you for the food on my plate, the roof over my head, the clothes on my back, and the love of my community.

But why am I full when another is hungry? Why am I sheltered when another is unsheltered? Why am I clothed when another is naked? Why am I loved when another is rejected? When the rain falls, the plants grow and, sometimes, worms drown.

Whelp, next we ask God for things on behalf of others.

CREDULOUS

Please, heal the cancer, stop the war, feed the hungry, comfort the broken.

And there it is. One of the ugly parts of prayer. Because you ask, you plead, you intercess and things change or they don't. Which is the probable outcome anyway. Prayer is the thing people do when they want to feel like they are helping, but can't. Prayer becomes passing the buck. Prayer becomes avoiding the truth of what is in front of us. Praying for the immigrant and the refugee means that I don't have to resist their exclusion from my country. Praying for the poor means I don't have to ask if my comfort has come at the expense of another's dignity. We need to sit with the dying, we need to acknowledge our part in conflict, we need to feed the hungry, we need to comfort the broken.

Like I said, I struggle.

Last night I had a conversation with my oldest kid, Laine. He had been sick all day and asked if he could take a bath and talk. The answer to that question is always yes.

Floating with his ears just out of the water, he asked me how my book was going and what it was about.

"Well, I'm writing a book about how God shows up in our lives and stuff."

"Cool."

"Does that sound boring?"

"No. Not really."

Then a companionable silence settled in the bathroom like the fog on the mirror. We were both thinking, I about this chapter and he about whatever eight-years-olds think about.

"Mom, what did you write about today?"

"Well, I tried to fix the first chapter so that it made sense with the fifth chapter, but I am supposed to be writing a chapter on prayer. But writing about prayer is hard." He looked up at me with pity in his blue eyes.

Prayer of the People

"Did you write about the Tekoa prayer?"
"No. Do you think that would help?"
"Yeah. You should tell them that your kids know this prayer and you can sing it with your friends. Then put in the words."

Then he went back to floating in the bathtub.

The truth was, I have been avoiding this chapter because prayer makes me uncomfortable. Prayer has been an exercise in guilt. A prayer offered in a moment of stress: you only pray when you need something. A prayer for healing that seems unheard: you did not ask in faith. A prayer offered in thankfulness: you are currying favor against the day you need to ask for something. Prayer feels like either self-deception or cosmic manipulation.

So, I decided to ask my son what prayer was.

And

He

Said

"I think prayer is being with people."

Just like that, he cut through all the emotional clutter and baggage that I have been hauling around for thirty-five years. Prayer is being with people.

Prayer is being with people.

Prayer is being with people as they grieve. Prayer is being with people when they celebrate. Prayer is being with people as they flee from their homes across turbulent water. I felt like the top had lifted right off my head. The understanding that when we pause to offer prayer, even if it is a wordless one, even if it is offered

CREDULOUS

from a distance, we are coming along side each other changes everything.

Everyone always told me that prayer was talking to God. What if prayer is being with God? In the story of creation, God mentions that it is not good for people to be alone. In the same way that God is, by nature, a relationship between the persons of the Trinity, we are, by nature, built for community. We are created to be with people.

But if praying is simply being with God and with people, and God is everywhere and I live in the suburbs, it seems that praying without ceasing might be easier than ceasing to pray. If my son is correct and prayer is being with people, then is sleeping on an airplane praying? If prayer is being with God, and God is in all and through all, then is it possible to stop praying?

Perhaps there must be an element of intention. *With* vs. with.

I am not a natural hugger. I am not sure where my arms go. Do I go over or under? One of each? What do I do with my face? How long, how hard, should I pat your back?

I have friends who have discovered this about me and take great delight in hugging me until I squirm. And they are jerks.

But there is something about a hug. It binds two people together in mutual, if awkward, support. And there is a moment of intention. One hand extended at waist level indicates a handshake is expected. Two arms out, body just slightly tilted indicates a hug. Oh geez, a hug.

Prayer might be a soul embrace.

Prayer might be allowing enough space between moments to feel the breadth of the germ of the infinite within you. Prayer might be considering the plight of another and being willing to allow them to settle into the safety of your soul. Prayer might be letting grace bloom into love and action.

Prayer might be creating space.

Prayer of the People

Or.

Perhaps prayer is potential energy. If a toddler climbs to the top of a slide,[1] the toddler now has potential energy. The force of gravity is giving the child the potential for motion even while sitting at the top of the slide. If grace is considered a force always in play, prayer could be the stored energy of grace. Once the toddler begins to slide, the force of gravity changes potential energy into kinetic energy. When a person prays, that person, who is being constantly acted upon by grace, is filled with potential energy, which can then be converted into kinetic energy when that person begins to act in love.

Prayer might be potential energy.

Several weeks ago, Laine asked me why his sister insisted on being a baby during every game they played. Context: Annabel is our second child and has been a middle child since she was eighteen months old. Two years ago she went from being the only girl to being the older girl. The girl without chubby cheeks and crazy hair. Annabel is affectionate, gregarious, and a hard-core introvert. She needs her space like I need food, and that leads to a fight between feeling isolated and feeling overwhelmed. She can feel unseen and overexamined during the same heartbeat.

Laine and I (an oldest myself) had a long conjecture about how it would feel to be a middle child, how it would feel to go from being the only girl to being the older sister, how it would feel to feel invisible. We talked about how important it is to allow people to be awkward right where they are and to make space for them to step forward into a more secure version of themselves. We talked about how wanting to be a baby was her way of asking to be seen.

Then a few days after that he asked me what being gay was. One of the audiobooks he was listening to had mentioned it, and I found myself in the middle of a deep and wide conversation about

---

1. Technically, the age or humanity of the object makes no difference for the purposes of the illustration, but toddlers are adorable and a ball at the top of the slide seems less adorable.

sexuality on a Tuesday evening at 8:30. Everyone knows that 8:30 is universal parent checkout time.

As we discussed that, "No, a man and a man marrying each other does not make them brothers," and, "Yes, I know people who are gay," and, "Yes, it is okay to be confused," and, as bonus information, "It is not okay to call someone gay in a rude way—not ever," he shrugged and said, "Mom, I don't really know if I understand being gay, but it seems like I should protect that."

Prayer might be offering protection: to hold space bravely for one another.

I have already mentioned a phenomenon that has been described in the physical world as sympathetic resonance. I first learned about it from my organ professor. Basically, sound is made of waves. Those waves have both amplitude (size) and frequency. The amplitude is the volume and the frequency is the pitch. My children maximize both. A child's shriek can curdle milk at twenty feet.

Anyway, if one sound with a certain frequency is played, other sounds at the same frequency or at certain ratios with that frequency will be amplified. There is a fun experiment you can do with a piano. If you lift the dampers (felt pads that keep the unplayed strings from vibrating) off the strings by pushing down the pedal on the right and play a low note, a hammer will strike a string. That string will vibrate at a certain frequency producing a predictable pitch. The length of the string determines frequency and, therefore, the pitch. The longer the string, the lower the frequency and pitch. What will make children (and adults who haven't lost their precious sense of wonder) gasp is that the shorter strings in the correct ratios with the string you just hit will also begin to vibrate. No kidding. If you can find a grand piano, you can strike a low C and watch all the Cs and Gs and various others at known ratios above the one you played begin to vibrate. This is called sympathetic resonance. You can actually see and hear physics. It may be the most satisfying thing in all of science and music.

Prayer of the People

I can't prove it, but I think there is sympathetic resonance on the level of the soul. I have heard words or ideas that have caused my full attention to swing around and face whatever it was. There are moments when something in me (my soul? my true self?) begins to vibrate like a struck tuning fork.

Prayer might be sympathetic resonance.

I don't find myself in church sanctuaries pouring out my words on behalf of the world anymore.
I am a bit more quiet and a bit more unsure, but perhaps I still pray.

Prayer might be intercessory presence.

8

Offering

IN ALL CHURCHES, EVERYWHERE, the one common functional belief and practice is the offering. Lights and paper for bulletins and coffee come from some place. Our common, shared responsibility. Our connection to what keeps life going. But in every church I have ever attended, the offering is seen as regrettable. Oh, the poor visitor who comes on stewardship Sunday—the apologies, the blushing, the regret they will have to endure. Apologizing for the offering is either admitting that the church is not using the money they ask for wisely or evidence of a complete dislocation from the connection between what we are doing and how.

Economics

Two years ago, Luke told me he was applying for a Master of Business Administration. He already has a Master of Divinity. Honestly, why would anyone need any other credential after mastering divinity?

But he had this nagging idea.

Offering

He kept saying that economics has something profound to say about the Christian life.

I thought he was having a profound midlife crisis. But he insisted that, no, he wasn't, probably, and that, yes, there was. He just had to find it.

House Order

I love cleaning. It is delicious. My favorite is cleaning floors. I am not terribly tidy, but I find it unfair if I have gone through the work of tidying a room and someone else wants to vacuum it. Acres of clean floor might be my love language. I can still remember the thrill of walking into the National Gallery of Art when I was nine years old and seeing the expanse of shining marble floors. Apparently, they also have art.

Laundry, however, is not my favorite task. I would rather clean bathrooms than put clothes away. I would rather eat kale than put clothes away. I would rather mow grass, clean out my car, reorganize the pantry, clean the oven, jog, or fill out IRS forms than put away laundry. Washing and drying I don't mind. Folding, while onerous, is satisfying. But putting the washed, dried, and folded clothes away is something I am never in the mood to do.

The problem is this: it is all connected.

When I find myself mowing the lawn while eating kale and filling out IRS forms while the laundry sits, piled up and wrinkled, I am denying that I can avoid the panic I feel when I am trying to find everyone's uniform parts for kiddo basketball on Saturday mornings or the quarter hours we spend digging for matching socks. I am admitting that the stress of putting clothes away is worse, for me, than the stress of disorder.

I hate laundry because it isn't sexy. It is boring and mundane. It is simply closing the loop between one day and the next. I hate it because there is a small part of me that resents that it mostly falls on me. I am already suspicious that by being a housewife–homemaker–stay-at-home-mom I am culpable in the promulgation of the patriarchy. With every load I do I see disappointment cross the face of the universal feminist avatar. *Which is probably an overflowing clothes hamper.* But, for me to be an educator-writer-feminist-lay-theologian, I need to put the socks back in the drawers. Because someone needs to do it. It is part of the system within which we all live.

Economics, as Luke explains it, should be understood as house order. The way the house flows. The organization and use of resources in a given system. Economics, or house order, seems to be less about the selling and buying in a society and more about the system through which the buying and selling is done.

Economics is buying the socks and putting the socks back in the drawer.

If I don't put the socks back in the drawers then there is laundry all over our bedroom and I won't be able to sleep well and then my writing will be terrible and you will never know the theological implications of laundry. Or economics.

So, there's economics as house order.

Complex Interconnected Systems

Jesus said he came to bring Abundant Life,[1] and abundant life is profuse, diverse, and interconnected. If you look at relatively closed biosystems, like Yellowstone National Park, you can track the influence of the introduction or removal of individual species. In the mid-90s, grey wolves were reintroduced to Yellowstone, and the entire system, from large predators to plants and waterways,

1. John 10:10

Offering

has been changed.[2] The entire system is interconnected by each element within the system.

The free market is a complex, interconnected system driven by an imperative of creativity and progress. For example, if you make Awesome Socks and I make Terrific Socks and sell them for the same price, the socks that meet the consumer's needs will sell best. If Awesome Socks are outselling Terrific Socks, I have three options in a free market: improve my socks, specialize my socks, or quit making socks. A free market relies on the trade of goods between participants creating a system of symbiosis and requiring trust.

In a capitalist system those with the most capital (buying power) manipulate the market by making and selling Pretty Good Socks from a position of relative power. In a capitalist system, sellers try to isolate themselves from their competition, not necessarily by making their product better, but by acquiring or putting Awesome Socks and Terrific Socks out of business. Capitalism is an isolated system of winners and losers based on power.

Systems that seek to gather consumers and isolate themselves from competition lose their creative imperative. A Methodist church turns in metrics every year to its administrative body for the sole purpose of making sure it is still engaging in God's ministry. And three of the most significant metrics that churches are required to report is weekly attendance, the number of people who have joined, and baptisms. We measure our spiritual impact on the world by the number of people who come into our particular building on Sunday morning. This is an isolated system.

If the religious community embraced a free-market system, intermingling ideas and constantly pressing toward a deeper, wider understanding of what it means to love God in this time and place, what effect would that have on our religious ecosystem? During this liminal time, the church must realize that we have embraced isolated systems, insulated by our doctrines, and decide what to do about that.

2. Dobson, "Yellowstone Wolves."

CREDULOUS

It is my view that until we begin to recognize the disorder in our houses of worship and find ways to reenter a free market of trust and openness, the decline of religion is inevitable. If the church embraced the rigors of diversity in our systems through intentionally seeking out dialogue with those from other traditions, how would that ripple out into our communities? Until we seek to repair the connections between those of us resident on our single known habitable planet, we will never truly see the economy of grace that Jesus talked about as the kingdom of God.

So, there's house order.
Interconnected, complex systems.

And then there's "The Why."[3]

The Why

Every business, apparently, needs to have a fundamental reason for existing, and the economics of the system should be organized to reflect "The Why."

Dog breeders understand this. For centuries people have been carefully crafting dog breeds, each with a specific why. Long pointy dogs are designed to get pests out of holes. Droopy-eared dogs are designed for following scents. And my dog was designed for cuddling. She even has soft fur and puppy-dog eyes. When you look at a German Shepherd (my neighbor's dog who was designed to alert the neighborhood to the dangers of delivery trucks) and a Cavalier King Charles Spaniel (my dog), clearly there was a long-pursued and well-understood why.

The why of the system drives the economy of the system. The why is the purpose for wearing the socks—are we going to play soccer or go to a business meeting? The house order for soccer socks will be different than the house order for business socks. Our religious communities must sit with this idea and listen until the

---

3. Sinek, *Start with Why*.

Offering

Spirit of God shows up with a particular why. Then, through connection and interaction, the why, or strengths, of each community can support the weaknesses of other communities and the weaknesses of each community can be met by the strength of the other.

So, there's house order.

Complex systems.

And "The Why."

Economics, baby.

Connection and Contemplation

How does economic theory, the order, the connectedness, and the purpose push us out of our spiritual apathy and isolation into a stronger connection with the call to loving community? Connection and contemplation.

A year ago, my husband signed me up for a spiritual pilgrimage to a small island off the coast of Scotland. We were going with the Missional Wisdom Foundation, we received partial scholarships, and my parents had already agreed to keep the kids. All I had to do was wean my last baby. The baby I refused to sleep-train because I wouldn't be able to cuddle with her forever.

I was not civil about it.

Unwary people would ask me about my upcoming trip to Scotland and come away wiping hiss and venom off their faces. Anyway, I went and it was amazing. I think I apologized for all the drama. If I didn't: I'm sorry for all the drama.

Pilgrimage is a walking process; there is a road, a destination, and a companion. Through hours on the paths and byways going to this place or that, the conversation flows around like joy. Pilgrims from different backgrounds and belief systems fall in next to each other on the road. Stories are told, confusions are aired, trust is tested out. As the miles pile up, so does the connection. This is the stuff of pilgrimage.

These miles of conversation suit me because I am an inveterate chatter-bucket. You might not know this because most of the time I manage to keep the chatter confined to my head, but something about Iona let it all out. After several days of walking and talking, Larry, the leader of our trip, spoke a profound truth into my life. *A few minutes of silence everyday would be good for you.* I think he spoke this in love and not simple desperation.

I did it. For over a year now, I have spent time being intentionally silent. There are brief moments when I can even hush the internal chatter. A practice of silence can be called contemplation. To live contemplatively, in the words of Elaine Heath, is to show up, pay attention, cooperate with God, and release the outcome.[4]

Contemplation is quieting the thinking mind consistently enough that one can learn to hear the kindness of the heart and the wisdom of the body. Contemplation is the practice of putting the spiritual socks back in the drawer so that when they are needed they can be gotten. Contemplation is economics in a robe.

Politics

Politics comes from a word meaning citizen. The unit within a population. If you are a citizen you must exist within a larger, interconnected system of citizens. That whole mess could be called politics. And, when politics and economics hold hands you begin to see the edges of something very important.

The Body

One of the metaphors for connectedness that Jesus used was the body. It makes perfect sense. A collection of distinct but connected, specialized units. Jesus, a first-century Jewish man, could not have known just how perfectly the body works as a metaphor of

---

4. See Heath, *God Unbound*.

community. The body is made up of cells. All of them the body and none of them containing the essence of the person. The person is an irreducible bundle of reducible parts. If the body in question is me, what makes it me? The dustiness of my shelves (which do not excite my cleaning interest like the floors) attests to the fact that lots of my cells drop off daily, dancing crazily in the sunbeams and settling on Brontë or Dickens or Moore (Christopher, of *Lamb: The Gospel According to Biff* fame), and most days I feel squarely me. With or without them.

So, if you were to begin removing your cells, one at a time, at what point would you cease to be you? Where is you housed? The body is a beautiful metaphor because we, as discrete units, do not comprise the kingdom of God or the fullness of the Christ, but together we can.

The problem with the metaphor of the body is that Christianity has tried to divorce itself from the body. Priests, the original keepers of Christian doctrine and definers of our faith, were celibate. I grew up knowing that, while the unforgivable sin is blaspheming the Holy Spirit, the eternally regrettable sin is premarital sex. While God may have told us to "be fruitful and multiply," God meant "with your eyes closed." We have a culture totally divorced from and unreconciled to our bodies. We are uncomfortable with ours and everyone else's. Our bodies are unwieldy terrestrial vehicles that crave to be sated with food, drink, and sex on a regular basis. Our primary goal in Christian life is to thwart the—probably devil-sent—urges of our bodies to transcend our pure spiritual nature.

I am; therefore I deny.

And deny. And deny.

Until you find me in the pantry eating chocolate chips right out of the bag.

If we want to understand God's economy or our connectedness, we must reconnect with our bodies.

The Gap

My husband and I like to sit in the bathtub after the kids go to bed. I hesitate to reveal this because it seems so private, but it is less exciting than it sounds. In the privacy of our space, surrounded by water, we talk about what is on our minds until the water goes cold. We talk about theology, the church, economics, politics, our kids, and ourselves. What happens after we get out of the hot-gone-tepid water is our own business.

It was during one of these late-night talks when he got through to me. I felt the pieces of economy, contemplation, and the body slide into place. I realized that we, as a society, can't feel our fingers anymore. We have let go of our connection to each other and the answer is economical.

Luke was right. Economics explains everything.

Economics is a system and practice that examines everything we do to make sure that it is in line with the fundamental why of the system. If there is waste or inefficiency in a system, the order of the system is unbalanced. If there is a disconnection between parts of the system, the integrity of the system is interrupted.

By ignoring our connectedness, the church insists that we live in a world where resources are scarce. The church doesn't act like abundant life for all creation is possible. The church has its truth, the church has its tradition, the church has its doctrine, and it must all be protected, or we will be impoverished. We, apparently, believe that, despite our religious language, there is no infinite God. Our house order reflects our ethos of scarcity, and we have learned to fight for what is ours.

My needs. My family. My people.

Offering

We bite and scratch like the violent primates we are. We go to war. We stockpile. We fear and shun and distrust.

And all to avoid poverty. Spiritual or actual.

And this economic disorder is creating a chasm between the church and the gospel. And this is where it gets interesting. This is where the body meets economy and creates Good News. It turns out that if we do not order our society well, if we do not pay attention to the economics of our culture socially and financially, we, as a collective, are less healthy.

There is even proof.

If the gap between the rich and the poor is large, then the health of all the members of that society is reduced.

This statement is based on information in a study released in the *British Medical Journal* in 1995. Over the last twenty years this claim has been tested and retested in hundreds of peer-reviewed articles. I have collected a few resources that I urge you to read through.[5]

It seems that once a country reaches a certain economic level, health and well-being seems to be inversely correlated with the wealth gap between the rich and the poor. And this is true for both the rich and the poor.

I am not sure we can say this enough.

We are all connected.

If the top 2 percent of your country earns more than ten times what the bottom 2 percent earns, and this discrepancy is not corrected through taxation or some other means of redistribution,

---

5. Wilkinson, "How Economic Inequality Harms Society"; Weir, "Closing the Health-Wealth Gap"; Institute of Medicine and National Research Council, *U.S. Health in International Perspective: Shorter Lives, Poorer Health*.

then the wellness of the society is decreased. If the rich are much richer than the poor in a given developed society, then the wellness of the population decreases across the spectrum of wealth when compared with societies with a smaller wealth gap.

We are all connected.

If the society in which you live allows the richest people to accumulate wealth without any effort to redistribute it to the other members of society, then both the rich and the poor are less healthy.

We are all connected.

We must choose to love God and neighbor because to do so is to care for our collective body. Not only do we all serve a different function, we are all needed for that function to be effective. And that is why economics is important. When Jesus said to love God and neighbor as you love yourself, it was not just a measure of how much, but it was an indicator of process.

In order to love yourself and your children, you must love your neighbor.
In order to be healthy, you must ensure that your neighbor is healthy.

We are all connected.

The economy of our health indicates that the gospel is really good news. It is good news for the rich and the poor. When Jesus told the Rich Young Ruler to go sell all he had and give it to the poor, he was suggesting a protective kindness for both.

So, Economics (how we order our lives).
Contemplation (through which we order our lives).
The Body (that which we must order).

Offering

The Kingdom of God

How we order our lives, in relation to each other, after the example of Christ, through contemplative connection to our bodies and to the collective body, gives us a glimpse of something: the kingdom of God.

Jesus loved to throw similes around when talking about the kingdom of God because no one understood what he was trying to say. I'm kidding. Jesus used similes when talking about the kingdom of God because the kingdom of God is an inconceivable, indescribable system of Divine order.

> The kingdom of God is like a mustard seed.
> The kingdom of God is like yeast.
> The kingdom of God is like a pearl, a field, a vineyard.

The kingdom of God is couched in metaphor, simile, and parable because it is so radical we can only see it out of the corner of our eyes. It is as paradoxical as being told that life can only be found through death.

It is an economic model from the dimension of grace.

The only problem is, we can only perceive three dimensions. All of our senses are tied to those three dimensions. Length, width, and depth. But there are more dimensions. We can talk about them, we can model them, we can even prove them with math I can't do (which pains me to say), but we cannot perceive them. But these extrasensory dimensions are there.

Which is just like the kingdom of God. We can talk about it, we can model it, we can prove it with statistics, but we cannot understand it fully. Just like we cannot understand the Divine source of life and love that exists in co-unity with itself and us, we cannot understand the economics of the Divine.

Jesus called being the people of God—the people of light—the kingdom of God. It made sense at the time. Actually, judging by the number of times that he tried to explain it, it didn't, but people were, at least, familiar with kingdoms.

> Jesus: "The kingdom of God is like some yeast."
> Everyone: "Huh?"
> Jesus: "The kingdom of God is like a landowner."
> Everyone: "Huh?"
> Jesus: "The kingdom of God is like a mustard seed."
> Everyone: "Huh?"

The kingdom of God is like a mustard seed. Jesus dearly loved the mustard seed. I feel like my spiritual education has been littered with mustard seeds. I have a bookmark with a laminated mustard seed featured in a tiny window. I was handed mustard seeds in Sunday School, Vacation Bible School, and youth retreats. I had a necklace with a mustard seed in a tiny glass bottle. Luke's first sermon ended with a spirited, triumphant, slightly confusing, "Be the mustard seed."

I don't even like mustard.

I'm a ketchup-only girl.

The wild mustard plant is a hardy weed that grows, irrepressibly, into large tangled clumps fringed with bundles of tiny yellow flowers. It is the foundational member of the brassica family. The brassicas are known to parents trying to convince children to eat something besides carbohydrates as super-vegetables. This makes them more amazing. Children are suckers for capes and alter egos. Super-vegetables are so nutrient-dense that it is worth begging or drenching them in butter to entice children or yourself to eat them. Over the centuries, people have, through selective breeding, crafted this wild wanderer into broccoli, cauliflower, kale, kohlrabi, cabbage, bok choy, and turnip. This is the legacy of the wild mustard plant.

The kingdom of God is like a mustard seed.

Offering

In first-century Palestine, a wild-growing super-vegetable would have been good news indeed. Brassicas provide the body with many of the nutrients it needs. It would have saved the landless poor from vitamin C deficiencies leading to depressed immunity and gum disease. This plant, free to all, unruly, and nutritious, is the metaphor that Jesus chooses over and over for the kingdom of God. The kingdom of God is like a mustard seed—a small bit of self-replicating genetic material that will blossom, yellow like the sun itself, with abundant, free nourishment for all.

The kingdom of God is like a mustard seed.

Which falls to the ground, tossed by the generous, hopeful, credulous sower, and grows to a very great size, then flowers, is pollinated, and goes to seed. How do the people of God turn empire into the kingdom of God?
I don't know.
Jesus the Christ, God incarnate, didn't give his followers a stepwise plan. He talked about seeds and fishing and breaking bread. He talked about showing up to where you are and noticing what is there. He talked about a God of seeds and soil. He poured his blood, sweat, and tears into his work, then left it to another. He taught that there was a farmer who came to sow seeds. The farmer dipped his hand deep into the seed bag and threw them out by the handful. He threw them out regardless of where they fell. He threw them out with gleeful, credulous hope. The seeds fell on rocks, on pathways, and on soil in great abundance.

In some places the seeds crunched under the feet of travelers, in others the birds screamed in delight, but in the soil the seeds found purchase.

Soil is more than the dirt we mindlessly walk on. It is history cupped in our hands, a song echoing down a century. Soil is the future following the worm. Soil calls through time and enchants those who pause long enough to hear. Stones are ancient and imposing but helpless against the grind of the future. Soil is a living thing that whispers of harvests while consuming the fossils of the past. When we lie down, finally, we will inhabit its tilth and join its siren's call.

In the garden, my hands cup the soil, drunk on possibility and the smell of warm dirt. Soon, I will lift my foot to the shovel, but just now, I will kneel here, in the ancient-becoming soil that will never be owned, and feel my soul sink down beneath the shallows. Down into the subtle depths where worms devour what was once a boulder. As I travel along the webs of mushroom hyphae, ant burrows, and clay ribbons, I allow wide-eyed hope to rise within me.

I return, season after season, driven by the same knowledge: somewhere—everywhere—in this dirt is treasure. Slowly, spring thaws to abundance and I am beckoned to come and seek once more. I become a sower of seed and I hope my extravagant optimism will bloom and fruit. Mostly it doesn't. Honestly, I am a terrible gardener. My failures have ranged from simply disappointing to horrifying. I have watched packets of seeds for children's gardens—"Easy to Grow!," "Guaranteed to Delight!"—unfold miniature vegetable tragedies. But still, I follow the call of the earth.

Yes, the kingdom of God is like a mustard seed that someone took and sowed in his field; it is the smallest of all the seeds, but when it has grown it is the greatest of shrubs and becomes a tree, so that the birds of the air come and make nests in its branches.[6]

Jesus said: the kingdom of God is like a mustard seed, which starts small and grows to a raucous, saucy, irrepressible size. How does the church become the kingdom of God? Probably like mustard seeds—flung out ridiculously.

For a while I worried that Luke was getting a degree in business so that he could understand the metaphor of economics (which seemed extreme), then I worried that he was getting a degree in business so that he could manage the empire of the church (which seemed wrong), and now I am worried that without a fundamental understanding of how economics connects us all we, as a spiritual

---

6. Matthew 13:31.

Offering

community, are in danger of totally missing the point. Economics changes everything. The question from the housed, fed, and clothed to the homeless, hungry, and naked becomes not "What can I do for you?" but "What do we need from each other?" Not "How can I save you?" but "How can we be transformed by God's economics?"

Consider the twelfth chapter of Romans. Romans was a long letter written to the newly forming community of Christ's followers in Rome. They were probably Roman citizens. Paul, who probably wrote the letter, was also a Roman citizen. The Romans were the elite class in the Mediterranean area in the first century. They were brutal, violent, weapon-driven conquerors, and *this* is what Paul said to them. It is important to note that this community would not have had access to the Gospels as we now read them. They would have heard stories about Jesus, but their main contact with the gospel would have been with the people who told the stories. And a letter.[7]

Dear Romans,

> I appeal to you therefore, brothers and sisters, by the mercies of God, to present your bodies as a living sacrifice, holy and acceptable to God, which is your spiritual worship. Do not be conformed to this world, but be transformed by the renewing of your minds, so that you may discern what is the will of God—what is good and acceptable and perfect.
>
> For by the grace given to me I say to everyone among you not to think of yourself more highly than you ought to think, but to think with sober judgement, each according to the measure of faith that God has assigned. For as in one body we have many members, and not all the members have the same function, so we, who are many, are one body in Christ, and individually we are members one of another. We have gifts that differ according to the grace given to us: prophecy, in proportion to faith; ministry, in ministering; the teacher,

---

7. Romans 12.

in teaching; the exhorter, in exhortation; the giver, in generosity; the leader, in diligence; the compassionate, in cheerfulness.

Let love be genuine; hate what is evil, hold fast to what is good; love one another with mutual affection; outdo one another in showing honour. Do not lag in zeal, be ardent in spirit, serve the Lord. Rejoice in hope, be patient in suffering, persevere in prayer. Contribute to the needs of the saints; extend hospitality to strangers.

Bless those who persecute you; bless and do not curse them. Rejoice with those who rejoice, weep with those who weep. Live in harmony with one another; do not be haughty, but associate with the lowly; do not claim to be wiser than you are. Do not repay anyone evil for evil, but take thought for what is noble in the sight of all. If it is possible, so far as it depends on you, live peaceably with all. Beloved, never avenge yourselves, but leave room for the wrath of God; for it is written, "Vengeance is mine, I will repay, says the Lord." No, "If your enemies are hungry, feed them; if they are thirsty, give them something to drink; for by doing this you will heap burning coals on their heads." Do not be overcome by evil, but overcome evil with good.

These are the words to the social elite. This is the economy of the gospel.

Be renewed.
Be transformed.
You are connected.
Love each other.
Let go.

We do not choose where and when and to whom we are born. We do not shape, entirely, the economic ethos of our country. But we do have a responsibility to seek to understand what our economic ethos is.

So, let us embrace the lessons of the offering. Let us embrace the economic, contemplative grace of the kingdom of God.

9

Doxology

Praise God from whom all blessings flow. Praise God all creatures here below. Praise God above ye heavenly host. Praise Father, Son, and Holy Ghost. Amen.

THE WORLD IS A harsh place.

If I am not careful, I can talk myself into shouldering the burden for the whole thing. I have a tendency to be emotionally responsible for those around me. I can, in times of uncenteredness, decide that I am not only called to love my neighbor, but I am called to save my neighbor.

There is a man that I know who walks through life without a family to support him. He does not have anywhere to go on Christmas morning. When he is sick, he must depend on the care of our church and his social worker to support him. This man has befriended me. We have experienced a lot together. When we lost our baby, he was one of the ones who embraced us. He offered nothing other than meeting my eye and acknowledging my pain.

He has known pain. He has known loneliness.

A couple of months ago he was scheduled for a surgery. On the morning of his surgery I felt like I should be there with him. I knew his social worker and a pastor from our church were going to be there, but I wanted to be there too. I felt I needed to be there.

I don't remember what happened, but I couldn't go to the hospital and sit with him. I wish I could say that one of my kids got sick or I broke my leg or my car wouldn't start. But I can't. I don't remember anything other than I didn't go.

Several days later I saw him at church. He hadn't gone through with the surgery. The thought of intubation terrified him, and he walked out.

I felt a lead-lined vest of guilt settle onto my shoulders. *If only I had been there. If I had shown him he wasn't alone. If he had known that he had an advocate.* I still carry that guilt.

He did not ask me to carry this guilt.

Should I have gone to the hospital that day? I think so.
But I didn't. And he still calls me sister.

When I saw him that day in the fellowship hall and he told me this story, I was busy berating myself for failing him, which was great because I was quiet. He poured out his fear, his suspicion, his need, and I met his eye and acknowledged his pain.

He taught me that the most significant thing that we can do with the suffering of the world is acknowledge it. Bring it into the knowing of the community. When I was in pain, he held me in a silent embrace, then let go. He let me know: you are part of me, and I am part of you. Then he let go.

And suffering?

Life is suffering.

The suffering of life is intense and, at times, unrelenting. The bearing and birthing of my children is something that brings me fierce joy and pride, but in the moment it was undiluted suffering. Two years after the birth of my last child I still get fatigued walking to the swing set in the back yard. And that is happy suffering. Life is also full of unhappy suffering. Suffering for which there is no silver lining.

When we suffer, we feel cheated out of happiness. We, after all, have the right to pursue happiness. When Thomas Jefferson wrote those words over two hundred and fifty years ago, he did not, to my personal knowledge, mean them as a curse. Obviously.

But to be dedicated to the proposition that, reading generously, all people have the right to pursue happiness is different than saying that all people have the right to happiness. Life is not happiness. There are happy moments in life, but there is also suffering. To deny that suffering is legitimate is to deny a good portion of life.

I have a friend for whom basic health has been a daily pursuit. She has had to devote almost thirty years of her life to courting her health. Her body is a jealous, demanding partner. I remember feeling the anger usually reserved for an abusive spouse as I drove her to the emergency room after a particularly deadly altercation.

One afternoon she asked me what she had done to deserve this particular brand of suffering. Always sensitive, articulate, and wise, I answered, "Life sucks; then you die."

Because it seems to me that you cannot embrace joy until you relinquish the craving for happiness. And that is the power of the Doxology—spoken or written praise that, sometimes, pours out of utterly giving up.

In the eleventh chapter of Romans the writer is wrestling with what Jesus Christ means for the election, the special chosenness, of the Jews. The Gentiles—non-Jewish Christians—were, guessing by the side of the conversation to which we have access, trying to say that God had chosen them, the Gentiles, to the exclusion of the Jews. For generations, Jews had been claiming they were the chosen people of God, and now the Christians were claiming Jesus had transferred that election from the Jews to the Christians.

The text dumps out a rather tangled and confusing welter of instruction that generally, in my best interpretation, says: everyone

CREDULOUS

is included. I have trouble with many of the epistles because they are written to a community I cannot comprehend and their language and references can seem dated, bigoted, and misogynistic. So, there is a lot in this chapter I don't pretend to agree with or understand, but the one thing I do get it this: the writer was frustrated. Perhaps angry.

He had tried to be clear and persuasive, but the people kept wanting a different answer. The people wanted to coopt Jesus as the defining mascot of their tribe when what Jesus said, over and over, was: those who choose to follow the way of love are all, even Samaritans, part of a new kingdom.

And so, when the writer came to the end of this argument, he paused and said:

> O the depth of the riches and wisdom and knowledge of God! . . . For from him and through him and to him are all things. To him be the glory forever. Amen.[1]

That is the very place to which I have come. Not out of frustration or anger, but out of sheer helplessness. I don't know how to address the likelihood of dark-skinned boys being shot. I don't know how to address the loss of manufacturing jobs and the subsequent collapse of America's blue-collar economy. I don't know how to address the rising temperature of the planet or the plastic content of the ocean.

So, I will give up and turn to Doxology.

I know that sounds exactly like what I shouldn't do, but sometimes giving up and turning to doxology is the only sane response. Or healthy one. Because when you are a fighter, when you want to see a more just world, when you want people to see past the differences that terrify to the similarities that unify, you must decide who is going to be responsible for the results. Is this all dependent on you, or are you living in cooperation with the story of love that is already being told—with or without you, but in a deeper, richer

---

1. Romans 11:33–36.

way with you. Because one of these leads to freedom and one does not.

When we give up and turn to doxology, we become free.

Jesus called us into a life of love. A life of loving God and loving each other as we, also, love ourselves. To love is joy. To love is to suffer. To love is to be.

We have come a long way in this narrative. We have travelled through the theological crevices of my mind. And now we come to the point when I must reveal to you: I don't know anything. And this is the place of wisdom that I have found after certainty, despair, and suffering.

I have been certain: the world was young, Jesus was our savior from hell, and I was born sinful.

I have felt despair: mine was not saved, I could not save her, I cannot save you.

I have suffered: I have loved and wept for it.

Now I realize that which comes after, because there seems to be an after or a between to suffering, is a wisdom of the Doxology.

> Grace to you and peace from God our Father and the Lord Jesus Christ.[2]

This is the wisdom that comes with suffering. I can't explain the brokenness in the world. I can't fix the brokenness in the world.

I give up.

I will try, I will witness, I will speak, but I will also give up.

This winter, just before the dawning of spring, the temperature dropped well below freezing. The flowering trees had already budded and some of them had partially bloomed. My husband and

---

2. 1 Corinthians 1:3.

CREDULOUS

I had occasion to drive through the mountain pass between North Carolina and Tennessee a few days afterward. The buds hung brown and sickly, translucent from their stems. The burgeoning color that had been emerging after the darkness of winter winked out. It seemed that spring would not blossom this year.

A frozen spring. Celebration turned to lament. Magnificat turned to Requiem. A world of chaos and sorrow. What if the apple blossoms froze? Apples grow well in our area, so a large portion of our industry depends on fruit trees. If the blossoms set too early, driven by unseasonably warm temperatures, then a late freeze can devastate apple crops, and, by extension, the apple farmers and seasonal workers who depend on them. What happens to the pollinators in our area if the trees don't blossom? Pollinators have become a known fragility in our ecosystem in the best of times. What happens when a large portion of their diet dies off just as they are emerging from winter hibernation?

The world seems a harsh place indeed.

But, miraculously, unimaginably, the trees still bloomed. It has been two weeks since the hard frost, and the weeping cherry tree that has stood brown and defeated in the cold has shaken out its lacy skirts and danced. Her petals are a bit singed on the edges, but I am all the more grateful for her blemished beauty knowing how close I came to losing it.

It is a wary exuberance. It is a conscious joy. It is a hopeful despair.

It is doxology.

> Now to [God] who by the power at work within us is able to accomplish abundantly far more than all we can ask or imagine, to [God] be glory in the church and in Christ Jesus to all generations, forever and ever. Amen.[3]

It is from this place, this wisdom, that the life of spirit emerges. Whether or not religion speaks to you, there is a place of spiritual expansion just beyond the struggle of your control. I talk

---

3. Ephesians 3:20–21.

Doxology

about theology. I talk about economics. I talk about community. But the truth is I must live from doxology.

I have a difficult relationship with Scripture right now. I am crushed by the smallness with which it is used. I am disgusted by the perversion of it into a weapon. But I am filled with peace by the words of the doxologies. They are sprinkled through the Scriptures as moments of release.

I give up!

Paul and I have some difficult history. His views of marriage, family, and women's fashion irritate me. Technically, I have my head covered as I write this, but it is in an ironic-hipster way. Also, I need a shower. Paul and I have differences of opinion on many things, but I have learned that, amid our clash of wills, he and I can cease our wrestling during these soaring moments of release. What if all my opinions are wrong? What if his are? What if I never find all the pieces to the puzzle? What if I never clearly articulate the grace I see all around me? What if I never address the injustice I also see?

> For from [God] and through [God] and to [God] are all things. To [God] be the glory forever. Amen.[4]

When God is the mystery in which and through which we live, we can begin to see the world from the place of Doxology. I will give up and give in to the grace that leaks, in freakish abundance, from the pores of creation—even from me. I am the emanation of a beautiful divine imagining. And so are you. So, let's all praise the Lord.

I give up on understanding.
I give up on control.
I give in to the power of Doxology.

---

4. Romans 11:36.

10

Children's Time

Jesus sat on a largish boulder, grinding some chalky limestone into powder with another rock. He was tired. It seemed that no matter how he explained things, no one wanted to understand. He bent down and grabbed a chunk of hardened clay and added it to the pile of gathering dust. As he ground the clay, its orange mixed with the yellow-white of the limestone. Idly, he mixed the colors together until he had a spread out a dust sunrise on the rock.

They wanted control. They wanted him to validate them. They wanted him to get lost in the minutia of the law when what they were squabbling about was the right to leave a human soul devastated.

"Is it okay to divorce your wife for any reason?"

If only that was what they had been asking. These men had taken the law and transformed it into something cheap and convenient. And where did these women, divorced and abandoned, go? What happened to them? They were left to fend for themselves, drawing water during the heat of the day, selling their bodies—their only commodity—and bearing the shame of the community.

These discarded women were the waste of a system that centered itself around those who could afford to talk about rules.

"What'cha doin'?"

Jesus looked up. There was an abundance of dirty hair and brown eyes staring up at him. This little person had one finger raised, which looked like it was contemplating sneaking into the pile of dust while Jesus wasn't looking. Jesus regarded this small figure. There was a smear of snot covering one cheek and the back of one hand. Jesus couldn't tell if the brown feet belonged to a boy or girl. This person was just standing, finger raised, waiting.

"Thinking. And, I don't know, playing."

"Can I play?"

Jesus shrugged. "If you want to." He didn't feel fun.

But the little girl, for it was a girl, didn't seem to care. She reached her finger out and drew a sun right in the middle of the pile of dust. Jesus smiled tiredly and added an absurdly simple flower poking up out of a line of earth. The little girl bent her head down close to the rock, shutting out some of the glare of the sun with her own slender shadow and added a flock of humpy birds. She had begun to smile and looked up into the face of this strange man who sat drawing in the dirt. The man grinned back down at her. She reached up and pressed a perfectly round dot on the end of Jesus's deeply tanned nose. Then she giggled.

Suddenly a woman appeared out of the crowd and grabbed the child's upper arm.

"What are you doing?" She scolded. "I didn't know where you were. You should know better than to bother this man." She began to brush at the loose garment that hung from the little girl's shoulders. Jesus noticed that the woman was thin too. She didn't look so much tired as worn. Her arms were brown and her hands were rough. He imagined that she was not a stranger to the gleaning fields. Shyly, she looked at Jesus, holding her child close in front of her. Suddenly, the woman smiled widely and she automatically reached out and wiped the dust off the end of Jesus's nose. Then she blushed a deep mahogany that made her look like a bigger version of the little girl.

CREDULOUS

"Mother, thank you for letting us play. I hope you weren't too worried."

"Thank you, Rabbi," the woman said, eyes downcast. "Come on, Sarah." The little girl didn't argue. She let her hand be taken and turned back toward the crowd.

"Wait." Jesus said quickly. "May I give the girl my blessing?" The woman stopped without turning and smiled down at her daughter.

"Yes, please, Mama," the small child whispered. The pair turned back.

"Yes, Rabbi, we would be honored."

Jesus put his hand, which suddenly seemed, to him, big and clumsy, on the little girl's head. He could feel her hair, matted and dusty, under his fingers. Her head smelled of sweat. It was somehow endearing. It was as if the child smelled like the tumble of play and the joy of the sun.

When he opened his eyes, he could see that there were a few mothers gathered with children. They all shared a certain exhaustion and desperation. They were braced and determined.

"Rabbi, will you bless my children too?" She was pushing three dirty boys toward Jesus. Two were looking at the ground, embarrassed, and the third was glaring at Jesus. Jesus smiled. He remembered what it had been like. Mothers always push.

"Mother, I will bless them, as they have blessed me."

For the next few minutes, Jesus asked names and put his hands on heads and felt the anger about his day melting away. He was filled with a wary hope. The dust he had piled up had been turned into a host of figures and butterflies and suns by the little hands all around him.

Suddenly he heard the deep voices of concerned men. Men he knew well.

"What are you doing?"

"Get those children back."

"The master is resting."

The women reached out for their quickly scattering children.

"But Mama, I didn't get to go."

Children's Time

It was a small girl. A girl who had not yet learned that she should not ask, that religion was not for her. Her mother shushed her and was almost out of sight when Jesus stood up.

"Wait." His voice was quiet, but everyone stopped and turned to him. He looked out at the gathered adults and saw their weariness and concern. He saw their realism and their fear. He saw their poverty and their guilt. He saw the faces of the children. He saw their interest and their curiosity. He saw their impatience and their energy. He saw their hunger.

"Bring her to me."

He put his hand on her head. She broke into a self-satisfied smile. She looked as if she might never admit that she wasn't allowed.

"This is it. This is the kingdom. Do you see them? I am not asking you to help the children, I am asking you to let them help you." By this time, a crowd had gathered. Jesus could see the faces of the religious leaders who had been making his day so difficult. "Unless you all become like children, you will never see the kingdom." He grinned and swiped up a finger full of dust and dotted the little girl on the nose.

That Jesus . . . he could really make a point, couldn't he.

I go to a downtown United Methodist church. We have a children's ministry and a children's minister. We have nursery and children's church and Sunday School. Some weeks, when I drop my children off at my church's children's programing, it is the only respite I get from childcare. And that is real, folks. There are times when I drop all my children off for Sunday School and sit quietly and clean out my purse. Because I can, because it's quiet, and because I don't want to think.

But from the children's bulletins to children's church, we have made it clear that what we do is "adult church." We excuse our disturbances out of the sanctuary so that we can have peace and quiet and, in so doing, risk losing sight of the kingdom of God.

CREDULOUS

When I began writing in earnest I did what all first-born, achiever-types do: I took classes. Our local college has a community writing program. Most of the other students were retirees. Boy, did they have great stories. There were stories of love, shoe-shine boys, old radio shows, horror, mother's recipes, and one about charging out into the night in underpants and a flashlight to face down a bear.

I wrote my submissions carefully and received my critiques bravely.

At the end of the last class, as we were leaving, the teacher asked, "Are you still homeschooling your kids?"

"Yes," I said.

"You should really stop that and write."

Certainly, there are people who know a lot more about teaching than I do. It turns out that it is hard to teach someone to read. But, this is why I homeschool: I want to be the one who helps them find answers for questions like, "Who were the people who lived here before we did?" (as in first people, not the two ladies who used to own our house with the extraordinarily green thumbs who created the fabulous gardens at my house, which I am desperately trying not to kill). I also love discovering that the square of each integer is separated by intervals of progressive odd numbers. One times one is one. Two times two is four. The difference between one and four is three. Three times three is nine. The difference between nine and four is five. The next square is sixteen—seven more than nine—and so on. I checked up to twelve times twelve, which is thirteen more than eleven squared. Oliver, who was working out squares with unit blocks at the time, failed to understand why I was scribbling and sputtering.

I'm not going to quit homeschooling to write, but my excessive nerdiness is not the only reason. I am convinced that living my life with children is a place of necessary grace. I have been able to do so many things by working hard, but I can't do this. Homeschooling my kids, managing their needs and quirks, means that every day I have to wake up and do something I know I can't do. Something that forces me to grace. The days I don't show up to them or to myself are ugly. I am sarcastic before lunch. They have taught me how to play and shown me how to be where I am.

When Jesus told his disciples to become like children, I am assuming that he meant for us to value children, not quit our jobs and eat only carbs and boogers. So, what is it that children show us?

Proverbs of Childhood:

- Flower petals should sometimes be picked by the handful and showered over your head to indicate that you see their beauty. Suffering does not nullify beauty; inattention nullifies beauty.
- A treat is sometimes so delicious that it should be shared even if you had to spit it out to do so. Sharing from abundance is nice, but sharing, willingly, from scarcity is joy.
- Pretending to be a ninja and being a ninja are only different outside your mind. You are the composer of your story. You can only be what you are, but you decide what that means.
- Protecting your brother is more important than your own body. There are moments in life when the most appropriate response is to launch yourself off the couch at the monsters.
- Everyone can be hugged. There should be no requirements for love just as there is no entitlement to love.
- It is always appropriate to wear tulle and sequins. Because it is always a good idea to embrace your beauty.
- Boo-boos should be shown because they were earned. Our experiences of life, beautiful or painful, are worth a moment of attention.
- Rocks should be thrown, sticks should be waved, and frogs should be caught. If you pass up the joy of this infinite moment, it is an infinite loss.

Maybe that's why the church always has such a hard time getting things done. The kingdom of God is a room full of kids with three-in-one adult(s) standing in the middle trying to get everyone to listen or line up or just stop screaming.

CREDULOUS

"Hey, put those matches down. I did *not* say you could burn your sister. I don't care what she said or what you think she is."

"Yes, you have to keep your room clean. Did you think I gave you this room so you could trash it?"

"Of course he can come in here. I don't *have* a favorite child."

Jesus must have known that children are intractable, selfish, and irrational. If God's kingdom is full of children, perhaps it is not the moderated, polite place we envision. Children are passionate, rude, rebellious, and uncouth. If Jesus had meant to say that the kingdom of God was full of children in some idyllic way, it would cheapen the likeness. If Jesus meant that people must be like children to enter the kingdom of heaven, he must have meant it in the fullness of who children are. Anyone who has spent an hour with children knows that they are not faultless. I have been a primary caretaker for children for nine years. Children are not perfect. Could that mean that Jesus's kingdom, the kingdom of God, is imperfect? Could it mean that until we become willing to claim the right of being loved while being imperfect we cannot enter the kingdom of God? I hope so.

A child's heart is uncannily resilient. They will be thoroughly terrified by thunder and venture out into the rain the next day. A child has not learned to moderate their voice or their feelings. They live with the credulous belief that their parent can and will push them on the swing anytime they ask. And a small child, one who has not yet learned that disappointment is as constant as time itself, will ask for joy even when it is inconvenient.

Is it possible that Jesus meant that the kingdom of God is a place of determined credulity? I hope so.

But, no. He couldn't have. Not with our God. The God who is so stern, distant, and angry. The God who holds sinners over an eternal fire. This God probably hates children.

Children's Time

After ten nights of tears and rocking, I weaned my last baby, gathered a bag full of clothes, and began a pilgrimage. My mom asked what I would be doing on pilgrimage. I told her that I would be going to the island of Iona off the west coast of Scotland (true), where I would be attending church services at the Iona Abbey twice a day (true), sharing meals with the other pilgrims (true), and working in the abbey garden (patently untrue). As previously mentioned, I was a bit resistant to going on this pilgrimage because: motherhood and babies and reasons, but I was also reluctant to go because I felt like pilgrimage was going to be either very serious and boring—full of the presence of a magnificent and stately God—or an unwanted return to the magical thinking I had so carefully distanced myself from.

I was terrified.

I am a Four on the Enneagram. If you don't know what that means, it's okay. The point is, I am prone to melancholy and fantasy. There are fictional worlds that seems more tragically real to me than Abraham Lincoln or electrons. In short, I did not trust myself to keep my self together on pilgrimage.

It takes two solid days of traveling to get to Iona from North Carolina. By the time I stepped onto the last ferry, which would take us across an ocean channel, I was physically and mentally spent. I had gone full-scale Wuthering Heights. There was theme music in my head.

It was dramatically misty and the abbey looked appropriately lonely and weathered. We were to end our arrival with a mile-long walk from the ferry landing to the hostel. I had worked out a suitably serious walking mantra, and, shrouded by my (mostly waterproof) rain jacket hood, I began the work of Pilgrimage.

I am here.

Here I am.

It was a mantra I had devised to keep me rooted in the real. My struggle with mental location sometimes blurs reality, so with every step I chanted my mantra of location: *I am here. Here I am.* It was the mantra of my pilgrimage. There was a bit of the existential and a bit of the practical. It ran through my head as the road met my feet five thousand miles from home.

We arrived at the hostel, which did nothing to dispel my romantic idealism, unpacked and walked out, mantra and rain hood in place, on a green plateau overlooking the ocean.

There were rabbits and snails everywhere. There were little tiny daisies covering the grass and grumpy patches of stinging nettle piled up in hostile conference. The beaches were covered in a rainbow of rocks. Red, green, yellow, white, pink, black, silver, striped, and some shot through with foolish gold. There were carmine anemones and vermillion and chartreuse seaweed. The water was five shades of blue and the sand was white.

If this was a place to go meet with God, God was not who I thought God was.

My mantra fell apart and I filled my pockets with rocks and turned to laugh into the wind.

When our week there was over, we walked down to the abbey for the leaving service. We read the liturgy, promised to take the word we had received into the world, and closed the gate behind us. The ferry pulled away from the island and I stood watching the shore as the car ramp folded up to close off my view. The people of the abbey were gathered on the wharf and, just before they were blocked from my view, I saw them spread their arms and begin to run in looping circles. They were flying. They were the wild goose, the Celtic symbol of the Spirit of God and Iona's signature. I laughed as tears dripped off my cheeks. The frolicsome God of the wild goose was not what I had been prepared to meet.

God is like a child: wild, free, and frolicsome, born on the wind and calling to all that this, too, is another day.

So, church. So, soul. So, self.
How, then, shall we live?
Live here, live well, live fully.

Like a child.

11

Scripture Reading—John 1:1–5

TODAY'S READING COMES FROM the Gospel of John, the first chapter, verses 1 through 5.

> In the beginning was the Word, and the Word was with God, and the Word was God. He was in the beginning with God. All things came into being through him, and without him not one thing came into being. What has come into being in him was life, and the life was the light of all people. The light shines in the darkness, and the darkness did not overcome it.
>
> *This is the word of God for the people of God.*
> **Thanks be to God.**

It all began with a word. When God gave permission to the light, when God called the light into being, when that first creative word was spoken into the singularity of a beginning, energy and mass bloomed into being: light. That same Word was born into the light from the darkness of a womb.

The Word, the calling forth, the naming of light, is a thing of joy and creation. Scripture is a collection of words that tell a story of light, confusion, failure, love, fear, and joy. It tells of grief and abandonment and it tells of hope and inclusion.

And these words have been used to exclude, control, justify, and abuse. The Bible has been propped up as the God-breathed, literal history and catechism of the Divine and, as such, God has been trapped in the unintelligible traditions and expressions of an ancient civilization.

The Bible is aggravating. It can be obtuse. It taught me not to raise my hand because I am a woman. It has caused shame because it turns out that bulldozers, not my faith, move mountains. It has taught me to pity those who do not know the way, the truth, and the life. The Bible had a happy ending for those who made it through. They would spend pristine eternity in heaven. But those who did not? They would burn in their shame.

The Bible has become *the* word of God for us, *the* people of God. It has become the constitution for the empire of God. We, as a group of people, are self-selecting as the people of our God. Now, I am assured by my in-house Master of Divinity that *us* does not belong in this phrase, but many times I think that it is implied.

Us, the people of God.
The chosen people.

We, the self-contained, strangely warm, self-assured chosen, claim this Word, this Gospel, these promises, for ourselves. Our privacy fences are made of bricks and stone and stained glass. If you choose to join us, then you can also count yourself among the people of God to whom this word belongs, but if you are not one of us, you will become an other: and others are terrifying.

Humans are social creatures, descended from persons for whom survival depended on being accepted into a tribe, and we are loath to risk tribal rejection and prone to tribal definition. There are the fun tribes: Duke vs. UNC, Cavs vs. Golden State, Star Wars vs. Star Trek. Artificial tribes to whom we can pledge allegiance where the stakes are low. And there are places where that which divides us is harmful: race, income level, education, gender, sexuality, religion.

Scripture Reading—John 1:1–5

Religious tribal boundary lines are dangerous. The body count is staggering and fear has made demons out of what lies just beyond our understanding. We make lists of acceptable behaviors and invoke our knowledge, hoping that we will somehow tip the scales of judgment in our favor. And if we have to thumb the scales by pointing out our *relative* goodness, real or created, eternal security for me and mine is worth a bit of honest connivance.

Religion does not seem to be interested in good publicity for God. Rites, doctrines, and laws have chiseled stone churches, temples, and mosques out of the unbreakable stone of rules and pathways and checkboxes. A lovely collection of homogeneous people selling baked goods for the benefit of those who are not like us. Our determination to provide some rationale for what we say and do has led us to create a rigid catechesis to define who God is and who God isn't and what qualifies as service to and love of our God. Our scriptures have become a divider between those who are in and those who are out: the narrow path of salvation, the stiff arm of doctrine, held out to keep us safely in the right. If you want our love and community, you have to check your uncertainty and otherness at the door because we won't harbor your questions or your doubt or your differences here.

I put the Bible down a long time ago. The years without a Daily Quiet Time are piling up. But, when I want to say something, when I am trying to explain why hearing my children sing makes me cry, when I am trying to translate the feeling I get when I am sitting on my porch watching a dozen kinds of butterflies feasting from tiny floral goblets, I reach for Scripture. Even with all of its inconsistencies and the pain it has caused, parts of Scripture make my whole self sing. It is in the Scriptures that I find permission to cast into the deep water, I hear that my body, made in the image of God, is very good, and I find, when I sit quietly enough, its stories rise within me like a bush full of butterflies.

North of Israel is an area that was known during the time that the Gospels were written as Tyre and Sidon. They were coastal cities, renowned for commerce and purple dye. But it was not the promised land. It was on the back side of Samaria, for heaven's sake. There is a story about Jesus "going away" there. Perhaps it was as a refugee from the religious community he had enraged, or possibly he was there to rest. But, it seems clear from the story that he was not there on official business. He wasn't wearing a stole or a collar, and his robe was strictly non-clerical. While he was there, a Canaanite woman came to him. To my best knowledge, the Canaanites were the people that originally lived in Israel. They were the ones whom God helped the nation of Israel, former slaves in Egypt, kill. Down to the animals. But their land was straight up flowing with milk and honey, so clearly God meant the chosen people to have it.

Jesus, a Jewish teacher, travels out of the Promised Land into the northern territory, where the (possibly) generationally displaced Canaanite woman lives. Her daughter is sick with something untraditional enough to be called demon possession, and this marginalized woman asks Jesus to heal her child. And he ignores her.

She calls to Jesus. He doesn't respond. She yells at him. He keeps walking. She shouts, "Son of David! Son of David!" Son of the king, son of the conqueror, son of empire. He was to her what the Romans were to the Jews. "You, Lord, Son of David." Was her tone taunting? What it demanding? I don't know. Scripture doesn't say. What it does say is that Jesus ignored her.

Empire is that which controls, constrains, and demands. Empire is that which manages chaos and provides clean water. Empire does a very good job at building suspension bridges. And while empire is itself amoral—not immoral, amoral, not moral—empire operates to gather power and resources to preserve itself, and will conscript human actors to operate on its behalf.

Jesus, the champion of the poor, couldn't be empire. What would the liberals say?

"Lord, Son of David, please, sir." *I see you. I know you.* "Have mercy. My daughter is sick. She has been taken by a demon. Heal

Scripture Reading—John 1:1–5

her." Her tone was wheedling. It spoke of a thousand years of dismissal. *Your God may not see me, but I see you.* You came with your God into our land insisting that you were the chosen people, as if we could not see your God with our Canaanite eyes.

In that moment, Jesus was empire. He was the embodiment of the colonizer, the oppressor, the superior. And he was on vacation.

"Jesus, can't you do something about that woman? She has been following us for ten minutes." Peter's beard tickled Jesus's neck as he leaned in to whisper.

"I'm tired," Jesus sighed. "If I help her, then there will be a hundred more within five minutes. All she cares about is getting a handout." Peter noticed that Jesus's face was coated in dust. The sun had tanned his face into a dark mask and his black eyes stared out, just slightly unfocused. He looked spent and disconnected.

"Just tell her to go away then."

"I don't want to tell her to go away. I don't want to tell her anything. I just want to get something to eat and sit on the beach."

"Master, please, have mercy." She had fallen on her knees, her voice was pleading and her robe was filthy. Her teeth were black and she had a bag full of tiny fragments of faded purple and red fabric tied to her back. Her feet were bare and her toenails were thick and yellowed. She was not a noble savage, wise in the old ways of the land that the empire ignored; she was a parasite made desperate by hunger and neglect. She clutched at the hem of his robe, dusty but well made.

"Let go. I am just a stranger here. I came for the people of Israel."

"Help me, Lord, please. My daughter is sick."

Jesus was the face of empire to her. She was the face of need to him. She was everything he couldn't fix. He was everything that couldn't save her.

"Why should I help you? Why should I throw the children's food to the dogs?" Jesus was angry. He had tried to get away. This woman didn't know who he was or what he was trying to accomplish. She just wanted him to wave his magic wand and make all the suffering go away. But the suffering wouldn't go away. Jesus turned away from the wretched woman. There would always be suffering. There was nothing he could do.

"Even dogs eat the crumbs under their master's table." She meant it as a plea. Her voice was thin and whiny, but something happened in that moment. Something happened to Jesus. The Canaanite woman had claimed her place at the table or under it. She had insisted that there was enough for even the unchosen. Jesus saw something he had missed. The message he carried was like the bread on the hillside. Broken and carried out infinitely. The words that he brought and the Word that he was came from the mouth of a most unfastidious speaker. Jesus turned to face her. He knelt beside her and touched her filthy shoulder. Tears began to run down his cheeks. Here was faith. Here was truth. There was nothing he could do, but there was something they could do. He sank to the dirt and lifted her chin so that he could see her eyes.

"Thank you," he whispered.

Jesus came in subversion of empire, but he did so within the context of empire. Jesus came as empire to show a new way for all of us, including the faces of empire.

Who was born of a virgin? Caesar.

Who was the Son of God? Caesar.

Who was the Messiah? A Caesar who would crucify Romans instead of Jews.

Jesus the Christ, the Word, the incarnate, enfleshed, embodied God, was born into humility, vulnerability, weakness, and, ultimately, failure. When Jesus died on the cross, he became a messianic failure. He did nothing to unseat the oppressors. In fact, they won. Jesus, son of the Chosen People, came to be Empire poured out for those at and under the table.

That is what Word can do.

12

Sermon

"May the words of my mouth, and the meditations of our hearts, be acceptable to you, O, Lord, our rock and our redeemer.[1]"

How often have these words been spoken by the poor, exhausted wretch about to deliver the sermon to a congregation of dutiful, complacent, sleepy people? I have seen the desperation behind those words when the pressure of trying to speak life, doctrine, and peace into a chaotic world seems more than what Ordination can do.

Our son Ollie, who is currently five and has not grasped the finer art of pronoun use, asks Luke regularly, "How come you are taller than Mama, but her is older than you?" In his mind, there is something directly correlative between height and age. We have come to the place in our bulletin denoting the sermon, and, in our minds, there is something directly correlative between theological education and spiritual authority.

During every social gathering around a table, when it comes time to bless the food, there will be an inevitable moment when someone says, "Luke, you can bless the food; you're a professional."

---

1. A common prayer before giving a sermon, based on Psalm 19:14.

As if a master's degree and an ordination makes his blessing of food more effective.

"You must have a direct line."

"Put in a good word for me."

I am deeply, personally aware of the danger of religion without education. It is easy to develop some erratic and harmful ideas if you are not aware of the history of erratic and harmful ideas that litter church history. So, I am pro-theological education. I think it is a good and joyful thing to have clergy who have been thoroughly educated and examined. Science has taught us that discoveries are best made within an environment of peer review, and the church's ecclesial structure provides a kind of peer review that makes sure the teachings and doctrines of the church do not become warped and harmful (ideally). I am pro-ordination.

But just because a doctor can describe and treat a heart does not mean that a doctor's heart is better at moving blood around.

There is a need for and value in theological education and ordination. I will personally ignore anyone who claims that I have said otherwise. I believe that God, the mystery that surrounds us all, is equally available to all, and I believe, without inner conflict, that a person who has gone through the rigors of ordination has been given authority to create a space for increased interaction with that mystery through presiding over sacraments of grace.

But, let us return to those of us sitting here in the pews. I believe that some of the decline of the church is due to the laity (unordained people) relinquishing their responsibility to engage with works of compassion and grace or devaluing the spiritual significance of the work they do. I understand it. I have shown up to do good work only to be asked when the pastor would be there to do exactly what I was doing—only officially. I struggle with my inner critic, which constantly badgers me to append caveats to every paragraph. *I think these things are true, but . . .*

Sermon

I am a lay person.
I don't have that degree.
I never did the work to be ordained.

If I went back to school or began the process of ordination, I wouldn't need those caveats. I have wrestled with whether I want the authority of ordination or the freeness of laity. I feel some degree of guilt about simultaneously claiming to be a theologian and resisting going to get credentials to be a theologian. What if I am not doing it because I am afraid I'll fail or I am too lazy? That's possible. I have done that before.

It's possible I will go credential gathering at some point, but right now I am learning to call myself a lay theologian because I think that there is a great need for the lay people to claim their significance in the kingdom of God. It is time that the people, the citizens, the members of the body stop hiring out their good works and deep-sea pondering to the paid professionals. We can no longer diminish our responsibility to God's work in the world because we don't have the proper credentials. We are all called to cast our nets into the deep water.

When we decide that we, the laity, are unqualified to do God's work, we deny that the work is God's. When Jesus asked Peter to cast his nets into the deep water, Peter didn't have to make the fish, but he did have to drag the nets onto the boat, row out to the deep water, heave the nets into the water, and drag the fish back in. The kingdom is God's, the results are God's, and the work is done in concert between God and people through grace.

When some are:

Set apart.
Called to ministry.
Called higher.

Something happens.

These terms create an artificial divide. This notion that God, the mysterious Creative force of the universe, assigns some people to a higher level of calling while consigning the rest to congregational wallflowers is a caste system dressed up in its Sunday best, and it is a sneaky way for lay people to avoid the mundane tasks of the kingdom of God. You know, the things we are supposed to be doing for the least of these that we have hired a pastor to do for us.

John Wesley, the founder of the Methodist church, said we swim around in grace at all times. It is the spiritual equivalent of the Higgs field or the water in a fish tank. It is there. Always. Which means that everything we do, from making sandwiches to preaching sermons, exists within the context of grace.

You can't step outside the Higgs field and a fish can't step out of the water (except for my brother's goldfish, which jumped out of its bowl to its desiccatingly tragic end). Can you step outside of grace? If you can't, why should anyone try get into this kingdom of grace? After all, I don't make much of an effort to be in our universe, and here I am.

I am of two minds about this. First, I truly believe we cannot outrun grace, so, on some level, all things exist within the dimension of grace. Second, there are some pretty terrible things that happen in the world, and some of them happen on purpose. What I have come to is this: people do things that hurt other people and things happen for which there is no good explanation, and, although those acts and occurrences are firmly rotten and terrible, it still happens within the grasp of grace. Their location within grace does not mean that God condones them, but it does mean that God is present even there. When my baby died, there was nothing good about that, but what I felt in the valley of the shadow of death was the bump of a shoulder of one who walked alongside me.

If we all exist within a dimension of grace, then, to begin to live more deeply into grace, there should be a pressing in. In the pressing in is a realization that this is where you were all along and where you are going. As you walk or cast more deeply into grace, there is a deepening of the work of grace within you, and soon you will know that there is an infinite nature to what each moment brings. You will know that in all and through all is the spark of mystery that urges us toward love and hope and joy.

Sermon

Fantastic.

I promise I think all that is true, just like I think the Grand Canyon is grand and space is large. I know it, but I am not sure I know it in my body. I have never been to space and I have never scaled the Grand Canyon; I simply do not understand the scope of these things. All that I know is that through moments of silence and embracing where I am and what I am doing and having the courage to recognize that I share a part in the dance of mystery that is life, I can feel a sense of grace expand in and around me.

My husband preached a sermon yesterday that made me fundamentally rethink life. It was well presented, well thought out, and came from a deep well of preparation and education. He was bringing his best to the shore of the lake. And here we all are, on the shore where we started, following a man who has just helped a fisherman fish. We are all here, learning and teaching. Casting and being caught. His best does not devalue or negate my best.

There is a beautiful lake in the mountains near where I live. The water is cold and is edged about with grass. Its waters have harbored generations of fish, frogs, and turtles. It is surrounded by blue piles of mountains and skimmed by ducks, swans, and geese. I have seen a rainstorm sweep down the mountain and swathe the whole place in cloud. The cloud covered the mountain, droplets hanging in the air, baptizing trees and wanderer alike.

On a bright morning, you can see the mountains and trees reaching up into the sky and reflected down into the water. From the fulcrum of the shore, life is seen in duplication. Along the south shore there is a rose walk. On a hot afternoon, the scent of the roses thickens the bouquet of the lake shore to a musky, cloying effusion of nature and design. There is a playground where I have heard my children laughing. And unselfconscious laughter is the closest I have ever come to hearing the Spirit of God.

High above the surface of the lake, someone has erected a cross. It is white and studded with lights.

CREDULOUS

Is that what makes the place hallowed? Is it holy because we called it holy or it is holy because God has called it good since the beginning of time? Thin places are described as places where heaven and earth come close enough to touch. I think thin places are places where our expectation allows us to notice what was always there. And that same God, the God who is in all and through all, has called us all very good. As the very good of God, I claim my place, alongside the ordained, as a gatherer of truth and a bringer of hope. I gather the courage to cast my net.

13

Communion

The Passing of the Peace

"Please stand and greet your neighbor."

Growing up, when my brother and I would bicker, my mom made us stand, facing each other, and "say something nice about your brother." Or "sister." Whichever made sense. We hated it. So, we came up with a secret code. If we said, "I am glad you're my brother" (or "sister," whichever made sense), then, by prior agreement, it meant nothing. We were a tiny cohort of rebels. Banded by a single purpose. Unified by trial.

We totally had Mom fooled.

In a service of Communion, there is a script. In the script there are several movements. One is the Passing of the Peace, which can feel, to me, like facing my brother and muttering, "I'm glad you're my brother." It's hard to mean something when you are told to say it.

Passing the Peace is an exercise. It is practice. It is supervised hospitality. But, like my mother's exercise, sometimes it is working on us without our knowledge. When we pass the peace, begrudgingly or otherwise, we acknowledge the power of contact. Hand to hand, like a fellowship of adventurers, we pass the strength and encouragement of the Peace of Christ.

When my first son turned six, he had lived in six different houses. We weren't running from the law. Or aliens. It was all the typical stuff. We were renters trying to find the best place for our family to rest. We were moving for work. We were searching for home. I lived in houses with beautiful kitchens, beautiful views, beautiful waterfalls, and beautiful neighbors.

But, it was really hard to make friends, much less community, when we never stayed anywhere for more than a pocket full of seasons. I remember walking through my neighborhood when I was a new mother, praying that God would help me find a friend. I had quit my job to stay home full-time, and I felt very strongly that it was the right thing for me to be doing. I wanted to raise my kid by hand, and I was losing my mind.

The isolation of stay-at-home parenting is thick and powerful. I had chosen to stay home. I was desperately lonely. I had chosen to breastfeed my babies. I was desperate for a night away. I had chosen this life, and I had no idea how to survive.

During those first few months of parenting, I was living in a commuter neighborhood where you could run around in your front yard naked at eleven in the morning because no one was home. I tried to pass peace. I did. I took bread to my neighbors. I sat on my front porch. I wandered the hiking trails that cris-crossed behind our house. I dreamed about turning the neighborhood green space into a vegetable garden where people could meet. And, still, I did not find the connection I was looking for. Longing for. Because we are all made for connection. Even introverts like me.

Then we lost a child.

And, I decided God didn't really answer prayers like that. God is not a cosmic vending machine that can be activated into giving me E7—even if I do it right. Because I didn't see how God could care about things like loneliness if God did not seem to care about things like delivering my child safely into my hands.

So, I silenced my asking, but not my longing, because we are all connected.

Communion

When I was a child, I remember playing basketball on the driveway with my family. It was rare that my whole family could find a spare hour to play together. When we gathered there, together, without the benefit of talent, and played, I felt that those were the real moments. I could feel it. The air was different. It was as if two worlds had overlapped and we were all more vivid. I distinctly remember one of those moments overtaking me. We were all on the driveway. It was a weeknight right after dinner. We were playing basketball the way a child paints. Unselfconscious and joyful. The air began to shimmer and I knew this was a moment to pay attention to.

But I didn't have on any shoes. My mom kept telling me to go put on shoes, but I knew if I went to get shoes the moment would be gone. The little rocks from the broken asphalt hurt my heels, and I was afraid of having my toenails broken against the bottom of someone else's shoe, but I could not tear myself away from the heaven that had broken out over the normalcy of Tuesday night.

Longing for connection is something that is deeply embedded in me. This action of clasping another's hand and passing peace is important. Awkward, but important.

I am a good student. Usually, when a concept is described to me, it is mine forever. But, for some reason, physics has always been elusive. Lately, I have been reading primers and watching YouTube videos about relativity and quantum mechanics because I just don't get it. I can follow up to a point, then I am left, firmly, in linear time, wondering what is missing. What is missing from these theories, so profound and respected, that keeps them from popping into clear relief?

Sometimes connection can be like that. You know what you want, sometimes you taste it, but something is missing.

Sometimes trying to connect feels like standing in a rock bottom river with a gentle breeze and cold, clear, ancient water sliding by your feet. The sky is blue and the air is just warm enough to make the cold water bearable. Your net hangs from your vest and your fly is tied tight to your line. The trout and the air and the water shout that meaning runs deep in this place.

Then you realize that your hook is embedded in your shoe and your line is winding around your legs and there is just no way to get out of this smoothly.

How does one translate the abstract beauty of theology into the awkward clumsiness of the Passing of the Peace?

Slowly. Hopefully. Foolishly.

What passing the peace means, in the kingdom of God, is having the courage to be foolish enough to try again. When we pass the peace, when we step out toward each other, refusing to remember what happened last time, we embrace the mystery of grace that startles us into joy. And, it turns out, sometimes, when you step out of your door, another steps out to meet you.

Confession

Kyrie eleison. Lord have mercy.

For how many years did I beg for the mercy of God thinking that God was angry and that my atonement was bought with blood and sorrow? An angry God must have a reason to be angry.

Lord, have mercy on me, for I am a sinner.

And I *am* a sinner.

Christ, have mercy on me, for I am a sinner.

I do not deny it. I have sneered and wasted and envied. Envy is my superpower.

Lord, have mercy on me, for I am a sinner.

But, I am not only a sinner. It is not my starting place or my conclusion. I was not created in sin or born in sin. It is not my nature or my fate. It simply is.

Confession is a lost place in our lives. Perhaps it is because we declare our right to be innocent until proven guilty or insist that we are guilty from birth. We do not confess, because if we do we will be cast away, sinners that we are. Confession is a place of authenticity. Our projected images cry out that we are invulnerable, independent, unblemished, because we just can't believe another truth might be possible: that we might be guilty and loved anyway. To confess our sin, our folly, our pride, knowing we are loved, is joy.

I do not deny that there is evil in the world and that people do bad things on purpose. I know that Jesus talked about the kingdom of heaven being like a field sown with good seed that gets oversown by bad seed and the weeds are gathered and burned after the harvest. I know about the sorting of the sheep and the goats. I know what I am risking by saying this: sin is not what we need to be wrestling with. It is not the most important thing.

Imagine you are sitting on the edge of a new year. You are still carrying fifty extra pounds around, your budget is straining from too many last-minute fast-food dinners, and you get out of breath carrying the mail in. So, you determine that this year you will stop eating dessert, plan meals, and exercise for thirty minutes three times a week. You find a plan, you get new shoes, and you buy a bag of kale.

Statistics are against you making it past mid-February.

Because you are wrestling with what is wrong with you.

In the Gospel of Matthew, the story of Jesus and the crumb-begging Canaanite woman comes right after all the lovely stuff about the kingdom of God being nutritious, precious, and free, and right between two miraculous feasts. When she asks for her daughter to be healed and Jesus asks why he should give the food for the children of Israel to dogs (meaning this lady), and she says, "Even the dogs eat the crumbs that fall from their masters' table," she has issued a mandate to wrestle, not with sin, but with the Divine. In the book of Genesis, Jacob wrestles God to a stalemate and becomes the eponymous leader of the nation of Israel. Jacob looks square at the Divine and says, "Me too." The woman at the well asks where she can get living water and Moses demands to see God and the Canaanite woman asks for crumbs.

Confession is our place to claim our place at (or under) the table, knowing that while sin is, so is love.

And Jesus? What did he say to this woman? He called her great.

The Breaking of the Bread

This is not a good decade for bread. Gluten, calories, carbohydrates. Pretty much, bread is on the bad list. But, why? Because we live in an era of caloric excess. If you were living in an agrarian society, living or dying based on the annual rainfall and locust population, wheat would be a lifesaver. When you sow one wheat seed or berry, it will grow and multiply itself into a harvest of food and seed.

There are two things that keep me rooted firmly in the Christian tradition. Eucharist and baptism. When Jesus instituted the Eucharist during the Last Supper, making it, along with baptism, one of the two United Methodist–instituted means of grace, he evoked the power of the table. The power of the table is sprinkled throughout the Bible like meals throughout a day.

Jesus walked the road to Emmaus with some of his followers. They were reeling from the disaster that Passover had brought. Their teacher, their firstborn, had not been passed over. Like traumatized soldiers, they told the story, adding new details each time. Jesus was a good audience. He asked questions and murmured sympathy and outrage in equal measures. As they reached their house, they asked him to stay for dinner. He settled on the cushions with them, and when he broke the bread and blessed it, they recognized him.

Three men stepped into the shade of the oaks at Mamre. They squinted through the hot gloom at the tent that was pitched there. A man came out and bowed before them and asked them to sit and rest. The smell of bread and roasting meat soon wafted over their conversation. "You will have a son who will show you, again, how to laugh."

A nation of people, lost and afraid, stood in the scanty shade of an outcrop of rocks. They were hungry. The children cried and the babies didn't anymore. The excited chatter had dried up with their tongues. Who was this God who had brought them here to die? Tents were pitched, fires started, waterskins wrung out. Then a rumor started: there would be meat and bread.

They sat down, filled with expectation and doubt. Hope and despair. Hungry.

And the birds came. Fat and slow. There were whoops and feathers everywhere. The smell of roasting meat made a counterpoint to the songs drifting through the cloud in the sky. Children laughed and babies cried. And in the morning the bread came too, "as much as each of them needed."[1]

The table stands as a centerpiece of faith. The table is the place where we all gather, confessing our sin and joy alike. Eucharist.

For the last year and a half, my family has been eating dinner once a week with our neighbors across the cul-de-sac. It all began with fifteen inches of snow and a week of shared meals. We smoked a turkey, they made chili, and then we started eating leftovers. We

---

1. Exodus 16:18.

could not get enough. There was sledding and hot chocolate and snow cream in five flavors.

They are evangelical missionaries; we are apophatic intellectuals. They sing praise music on their porch; we read liturgies on ours. They have Bible verses on their walls; we have icons. But our lives are centered around the table, and we all have enough. We are an unlikely, joyful mess who found community and connection in Eucharist.

Even in the suburbs.

14

Benediction

Two decades ago, I saw three everywhere. Father, Son, Holy Spirit. Beginning, middle, end. Proton, neutron, electron. Mind, heart, body. Yesterday, today, tomorrow. Mother, father, child. I was settled in three. The triangle is the most stable shape, and my God was entirely stable.

Now, I am seeing plus-one and it is wrecking me.[1] What was once the closed geometric of the Trinity has opened into a hilarity of three plus one. I am the plus-one. You are the plus-one. It is the gospel message. What we have is now, and where we are is here. God is not standing far off, waiting for us to cross over to some other place, to fall down and worship at the edge of the perimeter of God's trifold privacy fence. God is the ground and the sun and the water and the laughter of the child running through the sprinkler. The stability of the Trinity has become the rhombus, the square, the diamond, and the trapezoid. And it is beautiful. Electrons have now been joined by quarks, leptons, neutrinos, bosons, their antitheses, and whatever someone finds tomorrow.

---

1. Duggins, *Together*, 5.

CREDULOUS

And now, in this puddle of disorientation, I have found peace in abundance.

God is abundant. Life is abundant.

So go, you possibly infinite array of particles; go and be where you are, enfolded in grace, and willing to believe in abundance.

Bibliography

Dobson, Andy P. "Yellowstone Wolves and the Forces that Structure Natural Systems." *PLoS Biology* 12/12 (2014). https://doi.org/10.1371/journal.pbio.1002025.

Duggins, Larry. *Together: Community as a Means of Grace*. Eugene, OR: Cascade, 2017.

Heath, Elaine A. *God Unbound: Wisdom from Galatians for the Anxious Church*. Nashville: Upper Room, 2016.

———. *The Mystic Way of Evangelism: A Contemplative Vision for Christian Outreach*. Grand Rapids: Baker Academic, 2008.

Heath, Elaine A., and John Kisker, *Longing for Spring: A New Vision for Wesleyan Community*. Eugene, OR: Cascade, 2010.

Institute of Medicine and National Research Council. *U.S. Health in International Perspective: Shorter Lives, Poorer Health*. Washington, DC: National Academies, 2013. https://doi.org/10.17226/13497.

Rutba House. *School(s) for Conversion: 12 Marks of a New Monasticism*. Eugene, OR: Cascade, 2005.

Sacks, Johnathan. "The Dignity of Difference." Interview by Krista Tippett. *On Being*, October 29, 2015. https://onbeing.org/programs/jonathan-sacks-the-dignity-of-difference/.

Sinek, Simon. *Start with Why: How Great Leaders Inspire Everyone to Take Action*. New York: Portfolio, 2008.

Tickle, Phyllis. *The Great Emergence: How Christianity Is Changing and Why*. Grand Rapids: Baker, 2008.

Tillich, Paul. *The Courage to Be*. 3rd ed. New Haven, CT: Yale University Press, 2014.

Weir, Kirsten. "Closing the Health-Wealth Gap." *Monitor on Psychology* 44/9 (October 2013) 36. http://www.apa.org/monitor/2013/10/health-wealth.aspx.

Wilkinson, Richard. "How Economic Inequality Harms Society." TED Talk, July 2011. https://www.ted.com/talks/richard_wilkinson.

www.ingramcontent.com/pod-product-compliance
Lightning Source LLC
Chambersburg PA
CBHW022111090426
42743CB00008B/813